THE
WHISTLEBLOWER

How the Clinton White House Stayed in Power to Reemerge
in the Obama White House and on the World Stage

ONE ROCK INK PUBLISHING

MARINKA PESCHMANN

The Whistleblower

First Edition
ISBN: 0987834304
ISBN-13: 9780987834300
Library of Congress information available upon request
Scripture quotations marked (ESV) are from The Holy Bible, English Standard Version® (ESV®), Copyright © 2001 by Crossway, a publishing ministry of Good News Publishers. Used by permission. All rights reserved. Scripture quotations noted as (NIV) are taken from THE HOLY BIBLE, NEW INTERNATIONAL VERSION® (NIV®), Copyright © 1973, 1978, 1984, 2011 by Biblica, Inc.™ Used by permission. All rights reserved worldwide. Scripture quotations noted as (AMP) are taken from the Amplified® Bible, Copyright © 1954, 1958, 1962, 1964, 1965, 1987 by The Lockman Foundation. Used by permission. Scripture verses noted as (NKJV) are taken from the New King James Version. Copyright © 1982 by Thomas Nelson, Inc. Used by permission. All rights reserved. All Bible scriptures may be found at: biblegateway.com.
Published by **One Rock Ink** Publishing
Canada

Printed in the United States of America

Dedication

To Matt Drudge of the *Drudge Report*, and the author of the *Drudge Manifesto*. And to all whistleblowers and truth-tellers who stand tall in the face of adversity and deception.

"Take no part in the unfruitful works of darkness, but instead expose them."

—Ephesians 5:11 (ESV)

Table of Contents

Prologue

Once upon a time, the United States of America was one Nation under God, indivisible, with liberty and justice for all. Today America is a divided country with fading freedom and selective justice. Congress rams legislation into law without reading it. Elected officials, choosing power over principle, act as if they are above the law, with no accountability or consequences for their actions. Good, hardworking, patriotic Americans are penalized and smeared, while the corrupt and incompetent are rewarded. God-fearing people are mocked, while others worship at the false altar of celebrity, money, and politics seeking salvation that never comes.

Americans are waking up, disillusioned by the Obama administration's transformation of America. Candidate for president Barack Obama told voters that's what he would do. "Change" is what he promised. He is accomplishing his promise by using the tactics of Saul Alinsky, the father of community organizing and author of *Rules for Radicals*—the guidebook to pushing a progressive, social justice way of life onto America, where the "ends justify the means." In Alinsky's view and that of his acolytes, progressive social justice is the redistribution of wealth and the primacy of the societal good over individual liberty. His teachings are the blueprint for President Obama's "hope and change" agenda. Alinsky's book, dedicated to "the first radical known to man—Lucifer,"[1] became the inspiration for several leftist politicians.

History is repeating itself. The Clinton White House followed the Alinsky methods.[2]

As more Americans worry about their futures, and the future of their country, we must look at the past to understand the present, so we can make informed decisions about our future.

If you wonder how the disgraced and scandal-ridden Clinton White House dodged indictments in the 1990s and reemerged in the increasingly scandal-ridden Obama administration in 2009; if you wonder how the Obama administration will dodge indictments, keep reading.

When I started writing this book, I thought I would be telling the story of how Linda Tripp (who served in Bill Clinton's Oval Office and Hillary's counsel office), transformed from a dutiful employee into a crusading right-wing whistleblower, who almost toppled a sitting President of the United States. Instead, I found myself writing a different book entirely— an account of how the Clinton White House clung to power to reemerge on the world stage and in the Obama administration. This book chronicles the strategies and tactics the Clintons used during the 1990s' investigations and beyond to stay in power. They are the same tactics the Obama administration is using today.

During Hillary's 2008 failed bid for the presidency, author and social commentator Camille Paglia noted, "For all the claims of media bias and ill treatment by her male fellow candidates, Hillary has got off absurdly softly in this campaign. No one—neither her rivals nor mainstream journalists—has had the guts to explore or even list the bursting catalogue of past Clinton scandals, in which Hillary was nearly always hip deep."[3]

Paglia is right. It's time to vet the administration and the "ends justifies the means" ideology serving in the Obama White House that seeks re-election.

While I use the experiences and insights of Linda Tripp to portray the Clintons as they really are, Republicans and Democrats alike misread the Clinton era. Linda Tripp was not a whistleblower. She was an enabler; a woman who acted out of fear and self-preservation rather than a sense of obligation to justice. Thus in this narrative, she became the means to an end.

When Hillary and Bill Clinton vacated the White House, they left the way they had entered: dodging scandals and indictments from Whitewater to Pardongate. Many believed it was impossible for the Clintons to rehabilitate their image and return to power. "It's time to move on ... the Clintons are old news," became conventional thinking.

Thus, Clinton investigations ceased. Deals were struck with special prosecutors. Bi-partisan hands were extended in the spirit of goodwill. Hillary and Bill Clinton rewrote history in their autobiographies, *Living History* and *My Life*.[4] Bill launched his Clinton Global Initiative to "solve" the world's most pressing problems. Hillary ran for President.

It was a gross miscalculation to underestimate the Clintons. They are back with the Obama administration, in what has arguably shaped up to be the Clintons' third presidency.[5] Virtually every major position in the Obama administration has been filled by someone involved with the 1990s Clinton White House.[6] Hillary directs foreign policy as Secretary of State; and Bill Clinton has become, according to *MSNBC* the "President of the World."[7]

As British Statesman and philosopher Edmund Burke once said, "Those who don't know history are destined to repeat it." Yet, scores of people have forgotten how individual Americans like Linda were targeted, smeared, vilified, and indicted for speaking some truth about the Clinton White House. The Obama administration is like the Clinton White House on steroids. The administration is using the same Clintonesque-Alinsky tactics, except the Obama regime takes these tactics further; rather than targeting and smearing individuals, entire segments of the population are under attack. Tea Party patriots, conservatives, capitalists, the military, and anyone who disagrees with the Obama administration's big government policies is vilified. This will not end until their Progressive-Alinsky way of "governing" is exposed, because whether the 2012 Democratic Presidential nominee is Barack Obama, Hillary Clinton, or another Democrat, the same players who share the same ideology will be involved.

Had this story been told years ago—by those in the know, had they blown the whistle—it could have changed the course of American history.

After reading *The Whistleblower* you will know why they remained silent. You will learn how to stand up against corruption, stop the selective justice and special rights system that benefits Washington's ruling elite, and begin the restoration of the rule of law and honor that made America exceptional as "one Nation under God, indivisible, with liberty and justice for all." It is never too late for the truth to be revealed and for past injustices to be righted. This book is a cautionary tale of how what begins as a seemingly small benign act of accommodation can evolve into more involved and deeper corruption.

Linda once said to me, after enduring the politics of personal destruction and a criminal indictment, "If you believe nothing else, believe this: If the Clintons can do this to me, they can do it to you."

She was right. This is the book the Clintons, the Obamas, and those who share in the Progressive Alinskyite ideology never wanted you to read.

—Marinka Peschmann

Chapter 1: Under Siege

"What I feared has come upon me;
what I dreaded has happened to me."

—Job 3:25 (NIV)

At Union Station in Washington, D.C., I leaned against a massive white pillar and waited for Linda Tripp, until I saw her van fly by me and stop at the passenger pickup divide. I walked up to her, waving to get her attention. "I'm sorry," Linda burst out laughing. "I didn't mean to pass you by. I didn't recognize you."

I chuckled back. Linda was in a disguise too. She wore dark glasses and a chin-length black wig. *What am I doing? I should run. This is nuts.* I thought.

"The FBI got me this wig after they put me into a safe house days after the story broke," Linda said as she fiddled with it. "Hop in."

The words "FBI" and "safe house" robbed all the *"this is nutty"* thoughts from my mind when I climbed into her van. She put her foot to the gas pedal and we took off with the U.S. Capitol's marble column in our view.

Life before the FBI bought Linda that wig carried us back to January 1998, to when allegations first surfaced that President Clinton was having a sexual relationship with a former White House intern, Monica Lewinsky.

At the time, the Pope's five-day visit to Cuba to call "for freedom" headlined the news.[8] It was a historical moment because no Pope had visited Fidel Castro's Communist Cuba before. Meanwhile, back in the United States, an American civil servant's life, and the lives and legacy of Bill and Hillary

Clinton, were about to change. I knew what the public knew. I wanted to know what it was like behind the scenes for a person who lived through it.

It was early evening, January 20, 1998, when an unfamiliar white compact car had pulled up onto Cricket Pass, a quiet suburban cul-de-sac in Colombia, Maryland. The car parked across from Linda's home where she had lived since 1981. Someone hurried out of the car to her van and inserted a handwritten note through her window wipers. Later, a replica of the note was taped to her front door.

"Linda, call. Urgent. Must speak to you! Tomorrow is too late. Sue Schmidt—*Washington Post*," read the note.

As dusk dimmed to darkness that brisk snowy night, a virtual brigade of press descended upon Linda's home. Hordes of cars maneuvered through the dead-end street. Throngs of people elbowed their way closer. Flashbulbs flashed intermittently. In the frenzied urgency to get the next Clinton White House story, press crews unraveled their camera equipment onto the sidewalk. Their lighting kits beamed brightly over the glistening snow, aimed at Linda's house.

All night long, the press watched, waiting. Some wore night-vision goggles. By early morning, swarms of television crews, topped off with six satellite trucks, lined her narrow cul-de-sac. The media's vigilance continued for days.

Meanwhile, bedlam ruled inside Linda's home. The alleged Clinton pursuer was now the pursued. Sneaking peeks outside through the plantation blinds in her family room, panic and compounding fear ripped through her. She stepped away from the window as though knocked back by fire.

With the help of her kids, they frantically and haphazardly hung sheets over any uncovered windows in the house to try to block the media's gaze. Walking in lost, aimless circles, the Tripp family had nowhere to go. In the background, the family room TV was on, where commentary hissed and longwinded speculation about President Clinton's sex life provided repetitive, sparse hard-news updates.

"The world exploded on our front lawn," determined her then twenty-one-year-old son, Ryan, to his mother. He wasn't kidding. Three days earlier, on January 17, 1998, Matt Drudge's world exclusive had broken online on his *Drudge Report,* "*Newsweek* Kills Story: 23-Year Old, Former White House Intern, Sex Relationship with President,"[9] followed by: "Controversy Swirls Around Tapes of Former White House Intern, as Starr Moves In!!"—Linda's tapes.[10]

Since the *Drudge Report,* the intern, Monica Lewinsky, was calling Linda from various pay phones to tell her she was going to sign it—the affidavit in the Paula Jones sexual harassment case against President Clinton—denying she had had a sexual relationship with him, and in doing so, commit perjury.[11]

Judge Kenneth Starr's Office of Independent Counsel (OIC) Report tells us that at that same time President Clinton was calling his personal secretary, Betty Currie, and his pal, Vernon Jordan; two people who knew Lewinsky.[12] Then Currie, on behalf of the president, tried reaching Monica using their established code name, "Kay."[13] Hillary claimed she was oblivious until her husband woke her up on January 21 and told her, "There's something in today's papers you should know about." [14]

That something was *The Washington Post's* bombshell confirming *Drudge's* world exclusive: "A former White House aide surreptitiously made tape recordings of conversations she had with the former White House intern describing a relationship with Clinton."[15] Allegations of suborning perjury, false statements, witness tampering, and obstruction of justice closely followed. Linda, under a media siege, felt "like a prisoner in her own home."

Super lawyer Robert Bennett, the president's personal attorney said, "The president adamantly denies he ever had a relationship with Ms. Lewinsky, and she has confirmed the truth of that ... and I frankly smell a rat."[16] Former Clinton Strategist Dick Morris took a poll for the president and found, "They'll forgive the adultery, but they won't forgive the lying," hoping President Clinton would "sort of let the public down gently." Instead, Clinton responded, "Well, we just have to win, don't we."[17]

In 2004, Oprah Winfrey asked President Clinton: "Did anybody know? Did you tell anybody?" President Clinton lied again, "Nobody... I was all alone." [18]

Later that day back at the nation's Capitol, the then Leader of the Free World, President Clinton, sat down for a TV interview with PBS's Jim Lehrer. Confidently, and with no hesitation, he alerted the nation: "There is no improper relationship. I did not urge anyone to do anything that was untrue."[19] Back in Linda's home, she shuddered when she watched. She knew she was in so much trouble because President Clinton was lying.

The coldest chill racked her body when her doorbell blared yet again. Behind her double-bolted locked door stood another flower arrangement from the press, who'd been posing as deliverymen. "I guess they hoped I'd be lured to the front door for a comment," Linda said. But that night, paralyzed by fright, she couldn't move from her couch. She didn't know what to say to anyone.

An hour's drive away from Linda's house, a fax machine hummed. Ronald Pearlman's cosmetic empire, Revlon, rescinded its New York job offer to Monica Lewinsky (whom they met through a friend of the president).[20] Back at the Clinton White House it was damage control time again. In days, First Lady Hillary would serve as her husband's chief defender. Meanwhile, back at Cricket Pass, the media stakeout continued outside Linda's house. Later she'd learn how a savvy fourteen-year-old neighborhood boy had rented out his bathroom for $3 a pop for the immobile press to use. Smart. "He can probably put himself through college—twice." Linda said to me, joking at the insanity.

That January night, *Wake up! Wake up!* had screamed in Linda's thoughts; wake up from this nightmare. But it had only just begun. Now, helicopters were hovering above her house.

Desperate for silence, an hour into the media siege, Linda turned her phone ringer off, but thought she'd better check her voicemail. When she did, she found that it was jammed full. Message after message emptied out from people she recognized from television who called her unlisted number. "Hello, I'm calling on behalf of Barbara Walters," said one. "Ms. Tripp, please call Larry King at ...," said another, interspersed with frantic calls from her mother, in Morristown, New Jersey, who'd gotten cable TV for the first time in her life a week before.

When Linda heard her name on TV, she plunked down the telephone receiver. Her unsteady legs walked her from the kitchen into her family room. "I couldn't believe it," Linda recalled, as she had watched in horror and disbelief with her kids when she was given the wretched title: Chief Conspirator trying to take down President Clinton. "I was Public Enemy Number One."

As the shock and nausea penetrated her bones, Linda prayed—hard.

"God help me." She couldn't catch her breath.

———

In Linda's world time stood still. While the nation's opinions over the president split in half, Linda stayed indoors. Now a federal witness in a case involving the President of the United States, the once private citizen became a walking target. She and Ken Starr's Office of Independent Counsel (OIC), tasked to investigate the Clinton White House, were verbally gunned down by threats, fueled by an onslaught of accusations and condemnations. Some threats leveled against her life rivaled threats aimed at serial killers, spies, or terrorists. "You're a dead woman, Linda Tripp." "There's a bullet with your name on it—you f—ing bitch." It was such a devastating experience that she wanted to crawl up inside herself, roll away, and disappear. Others detailed her imminent demise. "There's a bomb in your car." "If it's the last thing I do—I'll kill you." A number of threats arrived by mail and were delivered addressed to "Linda Tripp, 21044," using her zip code like Santa Claus's North Pole.[21]

"It was unreal how the U.S. Postal Service found me despite the lack of a real address," Linda dryly recalled. "It wasn't because the papers hadn't published it."

The night Linda was placed in protective custody—into a safe house— outside of her home she had watched an ambulance with its lights turned off, sluggishly circling her street, the cul-de-sac where she lived. Never stopping, the ambulance repeatedly passed by her house for hours.

It was that ambulance which prompted the need for her to go into hiding, considering all the threats she had recently received. Linda was terrified of what this ambulance might symbolize, and her frightened thoughts skirted to the letter left on her Pentagon office chair, months earlier, when she was still a private citizen. "That letter was all I could think of," she remembered, recalling the shock she had felt when she had received it. It said, "Linda, Just thought you might find this of interest"—with no signature and handwriting she didn't recognize. That cryptic letter listed names of dead people who shared an association with the Clintons.[22]

As the ambulance continued its intimidating slow drive outside her home, like a macabre symbol of horror to befall her future, petrified, Linda couldn't sleep. It was about 2:00 a.m. when she snuck a peak through her blinds to see if the ambulance had left. It had not. If someone were trying to intimidate her it was working. Thank God her kids had been staying with family.

With rising panic, Linda watched the ambulance turn the corner of her street for what seemed like the hundredth time. Then she grabbed her phone and dialed her newly minted conservative attorney for help. He, in turn, notified Starr's OIC.

Minutes later, Linda's doorbell jarred her already-frayed nerves; outside stood four OIC agents. As soon as she opened the door, they raced inside. She saw more agents standing guard posted outside, fully armed, and ready to fire.

As most slept peacefully that night, an armed agent told Linda to "Grab a few things quickly. We'll get the rest later. Hurry."

"What about my dog?" she asked the agents.

"Don't worry. We'll take care of it. Please, you've got to come with us now, Mrs. Tripp. You're not safe here. Let's go." A heavy blanket covered her when the agents skirted her into an unmarked car, admonishing her to stay low.

That night, Linda was moved twice before federal agents finally settled her into the St. James Hotel, a residence hotel in Washington, which served as her safe house.[23] Her handsome room juxtaposed the ugliness she felt outside. Isolated, she was unable to leave for her own protection, and seeing danger everywhere she was climbing the walls. Every footstep in the corridors put her on edge. With nothing to do but worry, Linda ate with two hands and spent frustrated hours yelling "No!" at the non-stop television speculation coverage.

She later described her experience that night as surreal; living in a heightened sense of paranoia. There wasn't a lot of room for extraneous thoughts of mundane things—"like for banking or paying bills," she explained. Instead, a churning vacuum of disbelief ruled her. All she could do was obsess that if the Clintons, their aides, and Monica would tell the truth she could go home, and revert to a footnote. But that was wishful thinking. From her days serving in the Clinton White House, she knew how the Clintons operated to stay in power.

Meanwhile, inside the grand hotel people went about their business, oblivious that upstairs the Clintons' Enemy Number One was holed up. From the St. James Hotel's rooftop, one can see the Watergate Apartments where Lewinsky was secluded with her mother, Marcia Lewis. If you turned around, the White House focuses into view. Linda was in the middle, between the intern and the president the entire time.

The Clintons couldn't kill her, as their latest scandal grabbed the world's attention, so they did the next best thing—discredited her.

Did Linda really believe that Bill and Hillary would have her killed? I asked her.

Linda hesitated. She couldn't be sure, but she knew that nothing the Clintons did to hold onto power would surprise her. "I don't think the president or one of his henchmen is going to be behind a bush with an Uzi," she said. "Do I think it's possible that, down the road, I may walk in front of a Mack truck and have an unfortunate 'accident?' It's possible."[24]

For Linda, the repercussions of the fear she suffered through during the latest Clinton investigation were still visible, and kept her living in disguise. How long does it take to feel secure after being targeted by death threats? Does that fear ever go away?

No one in the world, and especially in America, should be afraid of their government the way Linda was afraid of the Clinton White House. As much as people may personally dislike her for tape recording Monica Lewinsky, she hadn't committed a heinous crime. The question that needed to be answered was why Linda felt she needed an insurance policy to protect herself from the Clintons. I brushed aside the reservations that had bugged me earlier on meeting with Linda Tripp.

Chapter 2: Meet the Clintons' Public Enemy Number One

"Ask the former generation and find out what their ancestors learned,
for we were born only yesterday and know nothing,
and our days on earth are but a shadow."

—Job 8:8-9 (NIV)

In December 1999, I landed a ringside seat inside the Clinton White House and Hillary's "vast right-wing conspiracy." It was shortly before the New Year's Eve ball fell in Times Square ringing in 2000. It started with a phone call.

At that time, President Bill Clinton was in the White House. First Lady Hillary Rodham Clinton was making history running for the Senate. Accused terrorist Ahmed Ressam had asked "an Afghanistan-based facilitator" to see "whether bin Laden wanted ... credit for the attack" he was planning (to blow up Los Angeles International Airport).

The man on the phone told me that my name was under consideration to write a book on a very high-profile person.[25] "This could be big. But there's one condition," he stipulated to me, "I negotiate as your agent. Interested?"

Having just completed a press junket, I was tired. On the road for weeks, I felt like a rock star without groupies. The enticement of dealing with another high profile person fell flat. For me, the sparkle of celebrity had faded many a story ago; especially after I had collaborated on the Hollywood memoir *The Kid Stays in the Picture* that *Vanity Fair's* Graydon Carter made into a documentary. But if it were a good story, an impacting story yet to be told, generally you could count me in. In this case, however, I paused. Agree to a condition on a story I knew nothing about? Ridiculous.

I stammered. He interrupted then blurted out, "It's Linda Tripp. She's ready to talk. I don't know what your politics are—" he continued talking.

I was no longer listening; my thoughts had zigzagged away. It was 1998 when Tripp had grabbed international headlines when it became public that she had secretly taped conversations with a former White House intern, Monica Lewinsky. Lewinsky disclosed on those recordings that she'd been sexually involved with President Bill Clinton in the White House. Clinton had denied the affair and was accused of suborning perjury, obstruction of justice, and witness tampering to cover it up in an attempt to fix a sexual harassment court case. First Lady Hillary had defended her guilty husband and branded his accusers, including Linda Tripp, as part of "a vast right-wing conspiracy" bent on destroying the president. In the months leading up to Clinton's impeachment, according to an *ABC News* poll, Tripp's polling numbers rivaled those of then Iraqi dictator Saddam Hussein, and chief terrorist Osama bin Laden, while President Clinton's approval numbers soared. [26]

It was the end of the 1990s, considered a divine time of peace and prosperity, when terrorism, al-Qaeda, Osama bin Laden, and jihad against America and the West made scant news. The perceived enemies of the Clinton administration, American citizens, however, made lots of news. Tripp's tape recordings, President Clinton's affair, and his 1999 impeachment were depicted as "the hunting of the president." The hunters involved were apparently driven by ugly politics, and, in Linda Tripp's case, also a book deal.[27] As the Clinton White House narrative instructed, the charges against the president were "politically motivated lies."

As the drama and political war unfolded, however, a problem emerged: the "vast right-wing conspiracy" was right. The president *had* been sexually involved with Monica Lewinsky. Tripp's recordings *were* accurate. He had lied under oath, and Linda did not want to lie under oath in the Paula Jones sexual harassment case against the president.

In 1994, Paula Corbin Jones, a former Arkansas state employee, filed suit against President Clinton. She alleged that when he was the governor of Arkansas, he had propositioned and exposed himself to her in a Little Rock hotel room three years earlier.[28] The whole sordid story was the talk of the nation and the world. Corbin accurately described "distinguishing characteristics" in Clinton's genital area. [29]

As for Linda Tripp, the mainstream press, following Hillary's persuasive vast right-wing conspiracy charge, had vilified her and accused her of being an evil snitch for taping her conversations with Lewinsky. Some members of the press seemed to despise her. She'd been, for a while, Public Enemy Number One; "With friends like this …" growled *Time Magazine's* Margaret Calson. "Friends don't tape friends, so could we all quit calling Linda Tripp anything but the spy-provocateur she is?" *New York Times* columnist Maureen Dowd decided that Linda rode on a "broomstick."[30] Other commentary was less charitable.

Was Linda, a former career civil servant and a single mom, guilty of trying to take down the president? The Clintons and their surrogates evidently thought so, including former Clinton Press Secretary Dee Dee Myers who described Tripp as "evil incarnate."[31] Was Tripp truly the most hated woman in America or was she, as *Fox News Channel's* Sean Hannity described her to be: "A hero"?[32] Or was newsman Geraldo Rivera's declaration that Tripp was "a treacherous, back-stabbing, good-for-nothing enemy of the truth," the more accurate description?[33]

"Enemy of the truth"—I had never liked that phrase. Having worked countless stories, I knew that sometimes the whole truth could take years to come out. Was that the case here? It was thirty years after the news of the Watergate break-ins that triggered the collapse of the Nixon administration when Bob Woodward and Carl Bernstein's "Deep Throat" became public.[34]

Linda Tripp had served in the first Bush administration and in the Clinton White House. She would remain in the history books as a key figure in one of the greatest controversies of the twentieth century: President Bill Clinton's impeachment. Yet, we had not heard her account of the events. Were those on the "Right" right or were the people on the "Left" right?

"Personally, I can't stand her," the man on the phone persisted. "What Linda did, taping a friend, was unforgivable." Unforgivable was another word I'd never liked. Hadn't Americans forgiven President Clinton after he had lied to their faces? "But it's an automatic bestseller. I'll call my lawyers—" he said.

"Wait. Slow down. What's Linda like?" I asked. "When did you meet her?"

"Well, I haven't but—" he stumbled.

During the Clinton years, threats and personal attacks from both sides of the aisle had split the nation, hitting a frenzied pitch when President Bill Clinton became the second president in history to be impeached. Controversial subjects are exciting and rewarding, but I was not ready to jump into a likely nightmare just because a book could be a bestseller. Like many people, I'd noticed what had happened to those who had crossed the Clintons and the Democrat party. They were smeared or indicted—publicly branded bimbos, opportunists, or accused of mental imbalance. Paula Jones came to mind, as did Billy Dale, the White House travel office director, who was indicted and then exonerated in Travelgate. [35] Even loyal Clinton staffers weren't immune. Linda's former boss, for instance, White House Counsel Bernie Nussbaum, resigned in disgrace. Long-time Clinton friend and former top Justice Department official Webster Hubbell was indicted three times and convicted in the Whitewater investigations. [36]

Across the aisle, Republican Henry Hyde was savaged and called a "hypocrite" for an extramarital affair that had ended thirty years earlier. [37] Both sides took casualties, and the Clinton controversies never ended. In 2011, for instance, current U.S. Secretary of State Hillary Clinton's top fundraiser for her failed presidential campaign was indicted for obstructing justice and illegally reimbursing contributions. Earlier, another Clinton fundraiser admitted to "defrauding banks of $292 million." [38]

Did I want to throw my hat in the political ring and meet Linda? Did I want to be involved in another political story when so many were already stuffed in bookstores?

"Let me think about it," I told the man on the phone and I hung up. Then I said a silent prayer. Over the next couple of days, I reached out to friends whose opinions I respected. All of them agreed I should go for it and meet Linda. At the time, the press had been fighting for months to interview the woman accused of trying to take down the Clintons. "But go incognito," I was cautioned, in case the allegations of immediate Bill and Hillary Clinton retaliation were true.

But there were hurdles I had to clear, including meeting with her lawyer. First up was a sit-down with her spokesperson. Linda's spokesman, a former advance man for the Department of Defense, had been speaking on

Linda's behalf for six months. At six feet four inches, the lean, fair-haired man had a commanding presence, even after he sat down across from me at a restaurant. He spoke passionately in Linda's defense.

"No one can imagine what she's been through," he said, blue eyes saddening. "If I hadn't seen it myself, it would be hard to believe. Linda's experience is completely different than what people think."

Over dinner, we flew through the usual writer rigmarole. He agreed I could write under a pen name, if I wrote her story. Linda was the public figure, not me. Pen names afforded me the freedom to pursue stories no one knew I had anything to do with. I liked that freedom, and did not want to lose it.

"Perfect," he said. "Linda wants to keep this quiet. She doesn't want the Clintons to know she is ready to talk."

Her spokesman had gotten my name through a well-known musician at a political function. It seemed amusing, possibly meeting Linda Tripp through a rock star, but then you would have to know the rock star. Years ago we had met in Los Angeles, during my celebrity writing days. For the last few years, he had become active in politics and causes he believed in.

We moved on to the next step: arranging a meeting with Linda. Everything was falling into place. Even better, he shared my desire to steer clear of the gutters, and Bill Clinton's sex life—a topic that had been re-cycled to death. I said, "I think people would rather read Linda's experience serving in the Clinton White House—"

"Linda is a registered Independent," he agreeably interrupted me. "It was never about politics or sex."

———

A blanket of snow covered the view outside my window when my phone rang. It was the man who hated Linda but wanted to be my agent.

"Linda's spokesman is out," he barked. "Call her new agent."

"What? Why?" I asked.

"He just is—" he snapped. "Here's the number. Call him."

I heeded caution and refused. If she were serious about telling her story, I figured, she'd get in touch with me.

A couple of days later, her new literary agent called me. He answered my queries in a competent manner.

"Should I bring in my agent now?" I asked.

"Meet her first. If it's a go, I can handle negotiations. Keep it quiet."

We went back and forth for days to arrange a meeting with Tripp. Finally, we settled on the date, and the D.C. area. But the exact location remained elusive. An aura of secrecy shrouded our conversations when another cryptic call came in informing me to expect a call from Linda the next day.

In the meantime, I reserved a car rental and plowed through heaps of research. I had no plans to bombard her with questions; I needed a chance to get to know her, but I had to go prepared. Many cases ago I had learned to withhold an opinion until I knew the facts. I tried to approach stories with objectivity; by putting myself in the principal's shoes, taking *their* walk. It was the only way I could understand why they did the things they did. Whether I agreed or disagreed was never the issue.

Linda knew much more about Bill and Hillary than President Clinton's affair. She had served in the White House and testified in the Clinton investigations from Whitewater to the death of Deputy Counsel Vince Foster. She also faced two criminal charges in Maryland for secretly recording Monica Lewinsky that could throw her in jail for ten years or stick her with a heavy $20,000 fine.[39] At issue was whether she had violated a rarely enforced Maryland State statue for taping her phone conversations with Monica Lewinsky. In Maryland it's a crime to tape record a person without the consent of all parties and knowing its illegal, unlike most states that only require one-party consent.[40]

The night before I was scheduled to meet Linda, I faced silence. Is our meeting on or off? I fell asleep not knowing. It was after 11:00 p.m. when my phone rang me awake, "Hi. This is Linda Tripp. Oh, I'm sorry. Did I wake you?"

"That's okay." I shook my head alert. "How are you?" She apologized for calling so late. She'd just gotten back from Christmas at her mother's.

The next day, driving onto the 95 S Highway headed towards D.C., a friend's warning popped into my head, "I hear Linda is the kind of person who makes coffee nervous." Time would tell. Mid-afternoon, I pulled over at a gas station in Colombia, Maryland, and dialed Linda's number. She answered first ring.

She directed me to meet her at a grocery store. From there, I'd follow her to her friend Kim's house. Kim, she told me, worked at *ABC News*. About a half an hour later, shielded behind dark sunglasses, she drove up in her wood paneled van. Cracking her window, she disarmed me with a broad smile.

"This is the first time in ages I'm not wearing my wig. I didn't want to freak you out," she said, holding up a hat and rolling her eyes. I jumped in my car and followed her. We eventually parked in front of a magnificent house. Although two years had passed since President Clinton's impeachment, Linda never left her house without wearing a wig, a hat, or other camouflage.

Standing outside the front door was Linda's friend, Kim. She rushed towards us. Quickly, she became Linda's protector, holding her arm while she ushered us inside. Soon thereafter, Linda admitted that Kim had never worked at *ABC News;* she told me that Kim was in the news biz as a precaution. It was unclear if her precaution was paranoia, an excess of caution, or some whacky, heartbreaking combination. But then who could fault Linda for playing it safe after living through what must have been a nightmare experience: pitted against the Clintons while being dissected, and judged by a global audience. In truth, Kim was Linda's media liaison and a trustee of the legal defense fund in Linda's "fight for justice against the Clinton White House."[41]

Most writers want to approach a story without a hint of bias or preconceived expectations, but often this cannot be avoided. It's a natural human reaction. As you research the story, you inevitably form your opinion. The key to combating bias lies in keeping an open mind, disregarding assumptions, and following the often windy path to the truth that frequently cannot be answered in a twenty-question Q & A format; because every now and then, when you're face-to-face with a public figure, you discover the person previously thought to exist does not but has been media manufactured. This was one of those times.

Linda was not the wicked, conniving ogre obsessed with destroying Bill and Hillary Clinton that I'd seen on TV. To the contrary, she was tense but also warm, and made overtures to ensure that I felt welcome. She looked terrific, had lost weight, and was smartly dressed in a fitted bright skirt suit. However, she gave me the impression that she was hoping not to scare me off. Was she seeing herself through the myopic media lens or worried that I was?

As we wandered through the get-to-know-you stuff, Linda began to relax. I tossed out ideas about how I thought her story could be told. "Shouldn't be political," I offered. "Everyone's sick of President Clinton's sex life. Let's take your walk back to the beginning, working for Bill and Hillary—"

Linda agreed. She volleyed her ideas, and was open to suggestions. Quickly, we found ourselves in sync.

Then, without provocation, Linda began defending her actions for taping Monica Lewinsky. I stopped her and asked her to take me back to the beginning of the Clinton administration. I asked, "What was Hillary like when you first met her?"

Kim silently shook her head. Linda's demeanor stiffened. Contemplating her answer, she'd begin a sentence only to drop it, in slow tortoise-like stammers, "There's so much—I can't tell you in—Hillary was—" She started fidgeting in her chair. The relaxed atmosphere we'd enjoyed evaporated, and tension snuggly wrapped itself around her like a strapping man.

Whatever happened, Linda appeared to be fearful of Bill and Hillary, and more of Hillary than of Bill. Did her Clinton fear begin in 1993 in the White House? Or in 1998 during the Lewinsky scandal, the obvious assumption? I wanted to know, but backed off. She was too tense.

But what she did say was that she'd never forget the day she first met the Clintons in 1993, when one beaming Clinton aide burbled: "Eight years for him, and eight for her. That's the master plan."

"Clearly a mere intern couldn't be allowed to undermine the 'master plan.'" Linda deadpanned. "And you can be sure it was utterly unacceptable that I, an inconsequential career government worker, might actually be believed."

Linda's "master plan" assertion came true in 2007 when Hillary ran for president and lost the Democratic nomination to Illinois Senator Barack Obama.[42] As of this writing, with President Obama's approval numbers falling, there are calls for Hillary to challenge him again in the upcoming 2012 presidential election.[43]

Cutting through the tension, I suggested we pick out a name for us to use whenever we spoke; hence the birth of my latest pseudonym, Pamela. From that moment forward "Pamela" was how Linda's family, lawyers, and legal defense trustees addressed me. In this celebrity-driven culture, people might think it strange that someone would want to write under another name; but Linda liked the idea. She was afraid the Clintons would sabotage any project she was involved in if they knew about it. The less anyone knew about me the better.

"It'll be Hillary's secret police again," she said. "We need to take precautions."

Did Hillary's so-called secret police—a term coined by former Clinton advisor Dick Morris—exist?[44] I didn't know, yet. Would the president and First Lady take measures to sabotage Linda? Seemed a little farfetched. Was Linda's concern outrageous? Maybe not. Consider during Hillary's failed 2008 presidential bid, "campaign staffers ... kept tabs on Monica Lewinsky ... to avoid any surprise encounters."[45]

Linda and her lawyers had a plan. They wanted her story out before jurors were selected for her upcoming trial, seven months away, in early July 2000. It was a daunting task, but possible, if I started writing immediately.

Having previously covered high-profile topics from celebrity stories to true crime, I once had a book deal fall apart after the principal went to jail. It was the movie producer and sports team owner Bruce McNall who served four years in federal prison for defrauding banks of more than two hundred million dollars.[46] When a person faces criminal charges, the stakes are high. I wanted to make sure that Linda understood the legal ramifications. Telling her story could vindicate her or hurt her case, and could potentially be used as evidence against her. It was crucial that what I wrote be accurate, though with no holds barred.

However, I also believed Linda's case was different from McNall's case. In that case, he pled guilty and was awaiting sentencing. The book was abandoned after a tug-of-war between bankruptcy and criminal lawyers and McNall went to prison.

In Linda's case, the possibility of a jail sentence was remote. Her indictment was based on a rarely prosecuted "murky" law. She maintained her innocence, and the OIC had granted her federal immunity for her cooperation in their case against President Clinton. Her criminal lawyer, Joseph Murtha, however, had apparently told her to brace herself for a conviction though she would likely win on appeal. She adopted a blasé demeanor, resigned to her counsel's defeatist prediction.

"Bill and Hillary can do whatever they want. They have the power. A conviction against me takes away from their misconduct. I'll be cast in history as the evil, convicted felon," she said. "They'll stop at nothing. You don't understand."

Not then, but in time I would.

On the flip side, there was a part of Linda that looked forward to her trial, because it would vindicate her. As she put it, "The truth of what the Clintons have done will finally come out in a court of law and not in the court of public opinion," emphasizing the gulf-wide difference between the two.

I noticed that whenever Linda spoke of her lawyer, her eyes lit up. She frequently credited him with her survival and trusted him with her life.

As far as Linda was concerned, the charges in her "bogus" criminal case were "politically motivated" to punish and silence her for speaking the truth and constituted an "abuse of power."[47] But if her case were bogus, why couldn't her lawyer quash it? Was he incompetent, or playing devil's advocate with a blow-the-roof off the courtroom legal strategy waiting to be revealed to the jury? Her story was becoming more intriguing. I looked forward to meeting this lawyer she so trusted.

Our conversation segued to a topic soon to become news: Linda's plastic surgery. Before facing the glaring cameras at her trial, she wanted to "feel and look like her old self." So she had flown with Kim to Los Angeles for a facelift.

"Looking like her old self," meant going back to July 20, 1993; the day Hillary's confidante and Bill's Deputy Counsel to the President, Vince Foster, was found dead in Fort Marcy Park in Virginia. It was also when Linda, one of the last people officially to see Foster alive, mounted her comfort food-a-thon. Within a handful of months, after Vince's death, she had expanded from her normal size 8 to a 16 and was "still growing" she snickered.

With a wink, Linda could poke fun at herself. She described how she'd "eaten her way into oblivion," then joked about promising that the next time she was caught "in the middle of a s–t storm with the Clintons and their spin machine" she'd "try to remember to get her hair roots done first."

Linda was funny, sarcastic with a self-deprecating wit. She didn't come across as the judgmental prude portrayed in the mainstream media, but I noticed that if I asked her about Foster's death, she'd clam up, and switch the subject to safer territory, which, for the moment, was taking pot shots at herself. "After Vince died, food became my only comfort. If it wasn't nailed down, invariably, I'd jam it in my mouth," she kidded, blinking the pain out of her eyes.

Time showed me how she would put up a strong front, using humor to conceal her pain. But the sorrow in her eyes betrayed her.

Hillary had ignited the brutal two-year war of words against Linda when she'd coined the phrase, "the vast right-wing conspiracy," casting Linda in the starring role.[48] A scorched-earth demonization of her character and motivations followed in the elite media. TV, radio, and print pundit "experts" also ridiculed her appearance. All that had worn her down. So much so, that she'd gone under a plastic surgeon's knife.

"Being the butt of jokes was no fun," Linda said, "I better make sure that the next time I surface, I don't look like a combination of Attila the Hun and Two Ton Tessie."

Hillary and President Barack Obama are Saul Alinsky disciples.[49]Among Alinsky's lessons, he taught: "Ridicule is man's most potent weapon. It is almost impossible to counteract ridicule. Also it infuriates the opposition, which then reacts to your advantage."[50]

Linda was visibly wounded after the lampooning and skewering, most notoriously by comedic giant John Goodman on *Saturday Night Live.* Although she conceded that Goodman's imitation of her was funny, with his over-the-top impersonation and recording-device flower lapel, she wanted off *SNL*'s punch-line list.

Linda's also wanted to show me pictures of how she had looked pre-Clinton, in 1991. Her pictures displayed a telling story. When I saw them, the contrast with today was stark. Linda looked like a different person—happy, carefree, and svelte. Serving in the Clinton White House and the politics of personal destruction had changed all that. Now, she was tense, fearful.

Linda was living proof of the destructive power of words. Words can feed wars and change hearts. Words can rip joy out of a person's life. The aftereffects did not end when the newspaper headlines switched to another topic.

During the 2008 presidential campaign, the politics of personal destruction reemerged. First, Senator Obama mocked "bitter" gun-toting, Bible-clinging, small-town Americans.[51]As president, Obama's Department of Homeland warned that veterans could be potential domestic terrorists, demonizing over twenty-three million military personnel.[52] Next, the media and political establishment vilified Tea Party patriots, a grassroots movement that adheres to the United States Constitution, by accusing them of racism. As Alinsky wrote: "The pressure that gave us our positive power was the negative of racism in a white society. We exploited it for our own purposes."[53] The demonization expanded to capitalists and conservatives; they were branded hostage takers, terrorists, and told to "go to hell."[54] Alinsky also noted, "A Marxist begins with his prime truth that all evils are caused by the exploitation of the proletariat by the capitalists. From this he logically proceeds to the revolution to end capitalism."[55] Public figures like Sarah Palin, Glenn Beck, and Rush Limbaugh were added to this growing list.

Finally, hours later, Linda consented to fully cooperate with me—candidly, warts and all. We were on. I looked forward to taking the reader inside Bill's Oval Office and Hillary's presidential counsel's office and clear up any misconceptions, good or bad, about the Clinton White House and how it shaped and continues to shape America.

Does a person wake up one day, roll out of bed, and on a whim decide to push "play" and "record" on a tape recorder to take down the President of the United States, or was there something that happened inside the Clinton White House that led to Linda's decision?

Less than a week later, Linda's plastic surgery story broke in the *National Enquirer.*

Chapter 3: Bump in the Road

"The discerning heart seeks knowledge,
but the mouth of a fool feeds on folly."

—Proverbs 15:14 (NIV)

"Two-faced Linda Tripp has a brand new face," blared the headline from the *National Enquirer* reporting Linda's plastic surgery that decided she looked like the "mammoth actor John Goodman in a blonde wig."[56] It was ugly.

It didn't make sense. Linda asked me to keep her plastic surgery under wraps and I did. Now her so-called new look was blasted all over the news. I called her, "How did this happen?"

"Well, umm," her voice was stern. An explanation was not forthcoming.

To be sure, Linda's plastic surgery was the last topic I wanted to discuss, but when you're trying to report an accurate account of the Clinton White House in a tight timeframe with a high profile insider who is facing "ten years in prison and a $20,000 fine," it's helpful to know if she intends to become "news."

Her plastic surgery story had legs. For the next month it marched onto several TV news networks including ABC's *Good Morning America, 20/20*, NBC's *Dateline, MSNBC*, and *Fox News Live*. Even late night television chimed in. "It's unbelievable," CBS's David Letterman joked. "I've seen the pictures and honest to God, [Linda] looks like a new man."[57]

When *MSNBC* joined in her surgery hullabaloo, they highlighted a *People Magazine* article that dedicated three pages, including a full-page photo, to Linda's "news," and credited five reporters in four cities for their reportage. The media's attention seemed pointless, except it initiated a recycled round of awful Linda press. With her trial date hovering closer, another spiteful headline was the last thing she needed.

On the flip side, making scarce news days after Linda's surgery story broke was the first attempt to sink an American warship in Aden, Yemen, on January 3, 2000. The al-Qaeda bombers failed when their boat sank, overloaded with explosives en route to attack the U.S.S. *The Sullivans*.[58] That failed mission foreshadowed future terror tactics that ten months later were implemented when the U.S.S. *Cole* was bombed, killing seventeen American sailors.[59]

Meanwhile, Linda was crushed. The media was back at her door wanting a comment and pictures. One night, with a depressed, blah tone in her voice she questioned out loud, "Why does everything I do implode?"

I didn't know why. "All I can think of is you need to look at who's around you. Who keeps giving you advice that blows up in your face?" I offered. She kept silent. Shortly thereafter her new representative, who was hired *after* her surgery, was gone.

Now into the first week of February 2000, five weeks had zoomed by since I had first met her. It was six months away from her summer jury selection, and assuming she wasn't convicted and sent to prison, there was another concern: the November 2000 presidential and Senate elections. Vice President Al Gore was running for president and First Lady Hillary had set her sights on becoming the junior New York senator. A story about Linda coming out near the elections could effortlessly be spun.

Keeping that in mind, I wondered what I was getting myself into. Would I even have the opportunity to interview her as her plastic surgery story dragged on and on, and she remained reclusive?

Best-selling author Bob Woodward once said something I could relate to when during his Watergate investigations he described how the story controls you, not the other way around. I was losing the prospect of reporting Linda's Clinton White House experience. I had to be realistic. Her plastic surgery media troubles and upcoming trial consumed her. Then, suddenly, to my surprise the story yanked me back in when Linda called me.

Finally, her attention was budging off her media surgery mess back to the Clinton administration when she revisited the topic of the Clintons sabotaging her. "Let me figure some things out," she said. "Then come here in disguise [so I wouldn't be identified as a writer]. Now you have an idea how the press is," she said.

"From a logistical portion, we can begin at my decimated hovel of a house," Linda suggested, "until we have a better arrangement." She was eager to move to Middleburg, Virginia, to dodge the press before March 29, "the next spike," which was another court date in the *State of Maryland vs. Linda Tripp*.

I was game to play by her covert rules, but concerned as the clock ticked. But hey, it's not every day I'd have a chance to walk inside the Clinton White House with an insider on their radar. I bucked up, and threw the dice.

Chapter 4: Honor and Privilege

"Surely he recognizes deceivers; and
when he sees evil, does he not take note?"

—Job 11:11 (NIV)

Imagine you're driving home, minding your business after a long day of questioning in a Clinton investigation when you stop at a traffic light. A tour bus pulls up next to you. The tour guide eye-balls you, then points you out to the passengers. Suddenly, tourists start snapping your photo, waving, some smiling, others are stern. Abruptly, you've become a moving tourist attraction. Imagine. Surreal, right? With Linda's self-deprecating humor, she recounted: "It was official. I was a Washington sight on the D.C. sightseeing tour. Linda Tripp was built in 1949 of German- and Italian-made materials."

Linda had picked me up from Union Station. Wearing our disguises, we were driving down Constitution Avenue in D.C. headed for the Potomac as Linda, an excellent tour guide herself, pointed out all the landmarks, like the Abraham Lincoln monument, as we passed them. Linda knew all the history, and reveled in it.

"Eventually, when I was promoted to Media Affairs, they gave me a parking spot closer to the compound," she pointed, as the White House came into view.

How did her greatest honor and privilege to serve in the White House become a nightmare?

For Linda it began in the spring of 1991 when she landed her first job as a White House West Wing floater under President George Herbert Walker Bush through her neighbor's help, a life-long Democrat who would go on to vote for Bill Clinton in 1992.

Floaters are virtually the only position in the West Wing where a non-political appointee serves alongside the president, vice president, and their most senior staff. A unique caliber of support staff, they serve as fillers who are expected to walk into any office without missing a beat. Often scheduled weeks in advance or booked for blocks, some floaters may fill in for lunch or cover when a West Wing staffer has an appointment or goes on vacation.

Seven months earlier, Linda's husband, Bruce M. Tripp, a career Army officer and a battalion commander, completed his tour at Fort Bragg, North Carolina. After twenty years of marriage, the Tripps divorced, and she moved to the D.C. area and got a Pentagon job. With training in executive secretarial work at the Katherine Gibbs School, Linda accumulated her work experience while living on various Army bases with her husband, as she raised their two children.

When Linda told her ex-husband she was applying for the floater position, he thought she was nuts to leave a solid Pentagon job with security. He had a point. Floaters are paid by the hour with no health insurance or benefits. Linda knew it was a gamble. She'd done her research, however, and also knew that in the understaffed West Wing, if she worked hard, she'd have her benefits back soon and went for it. For Linda, the notion of contributing on any level to one's country was a privilege. "How many people have the chance to work at the White House? It's an honor. I would've paid *them*," she frequently said.

Shortly after firing off a letter of introduction with her resume, Linda was scheduled to interview with Director of Presidential Letters Maureen Hudson, a twenty-year veteran who hired career federal civil servants known as "careerists" in the White House Office of Presidential Correspondence. Careerists work for the institution of the presidency as opposed to "politicals" who are appointed at the pleasure of the president. Most careerists remain until retirement. While politicals employ most positions within the White House complex, they change with each administration. Political appointees are loyal not only to the institution but to the incumbent and advance the administration's agenda.

Thrilled and nervous about her interview, Linda knew filling the floater slot was tough because competition was fierce, the scrutiny was unparalleled, and few slots opened up.

All that made her worry about botching the interview, that spring of 1991, on the ride into D.C. The bus dropped her off at the Old Executive Office Building (OEOB), the work-horse of the White House complex located seconds away from The Residence and the West Wing.

Bordering State Place and Pennsylvania Avenue, the OEOB was built between 1871 and 1888, epitomizing the wedding-cake style of architecture. Originally, it housed the War, State, and Navy Departments.

At the OEOB entrance, Linda checked in with the Secret Service agents, providing them with her identification including her social security number. After being cleared in as an appointment through the WAVE (Workers and Visitors Entry System) logs, Linda received a pink visitor's pass with an "A" to wear on a chain. She passed by massive oak doors with small brass plates indicating room numbers looking for Room 60 to go to her interview. In 1998, the WAVE logs served as evidence in Kenneth Starr's Clinton-Lewinsky investigation.

Maureen Hudson, attractive with a youthful appearance, interviewed Linda at her office. "As we talked, Maureen tried to put me at ease," Linda recalled, "but despite her warmth and kindness the interview was intimidating because it meant so much to me." Over Maureen's shoulder through the window, Linda could see the White House and she was tense. Overlooking unblemished green grounds, she saw a Marine guard posted outside the West Wing lobby, indicating the president was inside. Further down the north portico, a press standup began shooting. Then a limousine drove past the dull-black, tall iron fence decorated halfway-up with gold stars and eagles. *Which Cabinet Secretary was meeting with the president about which policy?* she wondered.

"I was so insecure. I thought I'd blown the interview," Linda recounted. "Why would they hire me, the hick from Morristown, New Jersey, when they could hire anybody? How could I be so lucky as to work at the White House?" But they did hire her. On April 29, 1991, Linda's dream came true.

That April morning anticipation woke her up early. In a few hours she was going to work at 1600 Pennsylvania Avenue, serving in President George H.W. Bush's White House. Giving in to her excitement-induced insomnia, she arrived early— this time, as a poised staffer. Still not believing her good fortune, she pinched herself. When she crossed the threshold of Room 60, Hudson emerged from her office, "Linda, soon you'll be across the street at the White House," she welcomed.

Hudson's assistant handed her a stack of routine paperwork for staffers to fill out, then they went to the presidential correspondence typing unit where floaters worked when they weren't floating. It's where presidential letters and Executive Orders are quickly generated in massive numbers; everything from copying proposed legislation to answering fan letters to First Pets. Some letters were sweet; *"Dear Mr. President. I am five. My dog, Sugar, wants to come to your house and play with Ranger."* Some were heartbreaking; *"My three-year-old son has leukemia. Please focus more time and money on cancer research."*

Maureen introduced Linda to other floaters and careerists, and assigned her a cubicle when they sat down. Between the clatter of word processing, the ladies swapped stories about their families, their lives. From Linda's vantage point there was no political agenda in sight. All served with distinction without regard to party. Some had served in administrations back to John F. Kennedy. Respect and decorum permeated the office.

The paperwork Linda was given earlier was the mandatory (for both politicals and careerists) White House employee security background questionnaire conducted by the FBI. It's the basis for their rigorous investigation to determine a staffer's level of security clearance. Linda had undergone background investigations before, including one at the Department of Defense for secret and top-secret clearance, and full top-secret Delta Force clearance in North Carolina. But to work in the West Wing, the FBI background check started from scratch. Until it was completed, and she received the green light, she'd remain in the OEOB to do whatever she could and do it proudly.

Security clearance within the Executive branch is determined by four key criteria: Character, Associates, Reputation, and Loyalty (acronym CARL). Often "loyalty" is misinterpreted as loyalty to the president, but it means loyalty to the flag, to the United States. Every five years careerists are re-cleared. At the time, it took roughly three months and cost approximately $30,000 per person to clear. When the FBI goes out in the field to document a person's character, they interview people from your past and present searching for reasons why you *can't* be hired.

Used by six presidents, the clearance objectives were designed to protect national security, the president, taxpayers, and the White House by ensuring that no staffer had done anything that could embarrass the president or hurt the country. Blackmail, addiction to drugs, criminal wrongdoing, harboring a hidden allegiance to an enemy group, a hostile nation, or an unpatriotic action meant no clearance and no job. Under the Clinton administration a new criteria was added to the security clearance: determining party loyalty. Previously, it had never mattered because careerists serve the institution of the presidency.

In 2008, questions arose as to whether Democratic presidential candidate Senator Barack Obama would pass a background check. Typically someone with admitted drug use and friendships with unrepentant domestic terrorists like William Ayers and his wife, Bernadine Dohrn, of the Weather Underground, who tried to overthrow the U.S. government in the 1960s and '70s; and Black Liberation theologian Reverend Jeremiah "G-d damn America" Wright would be disqualifying factors.[60] Presidents are exempted from these background checks.

Once the investigation is completed, the FBI file becomes two-fold: first, a file containing incontrovertible information, and second, a RAW DATA file comprised of unverifiable information, including hearsay.[61]

Information in the RAW data portion could be viewed as a fast track to the tabloids because it might contain names and numbers of people with questionable credentials or motives. In the wrong hands, RAW data could intimidate an innocent person.

The government's ability to recruit qualified and decent people largely depends upon the confidentiality of background investigations. Selected characterizations leaked from an FBI file could ruin careers and reputations, which is why it's illegal to release them. Perception often sticks before the reality can erase it and the damage is done.

An employee's level of clearance is represented by colored laminated passes hung on a chain that staffers are required to wear. Orange pass holders have access to the OEOB and New Executive Office Building (NEOB), and covet *the pass,* the blue pass. A blue pass with a "W" means unescorted access to the West Wing and the president. A blue pass with "RES" allows access to the West Wing and to the First Family's private residence.

A year into the Clinton administration some senior staffers still worked under temporary passes. Finally, some were let go because they were unclearable. In other cases, the Clinton administration intervened by creating a drug testing program after background checks revealed over twenty-one incoming politicals testing positive for recent illegal drug use. Cocaine, hallucinogenics, and crack were among the drugs used.[62]

"Is there anything in your background which could surface and hurt the president or the country?" Hudson asked Linda that day in April 1991. Her mind flashed backwards. No. She had to nothing to hide. Nothing in her past would prevent her from serving in the White House.

Three months later in August 1991 Linda's West Wing clearance was granted. She hung her coveted blue pass around her neck. Now, like other cleared staffers, with a flash of her pass to the White House gate guards she was in. She floated from the OEOB to the office of the Assistant to the President for Media Affairs in the West Wing. Linda's new boss was an award-winning journalist who had won five Emmy Awards while at ABC's *Nightline.*

Reporting to her first West Wing assignment, Linda's feet sunk into the plush carpet as she treaded through its magnificent corridors. Her romantic vision of the West Wing paled to the reality, as she recounted the quiet dignity and professional atmosphere that prevailed. The West Wing was surprisingly small and homey. It's a place where decisions affecting millions of people occur. "All I could think about was how I must be the luckiest person. To serve was such an honor," she said.

Around her were hurried conversations between staffers convened in hallways—hammering out policy. Dressed in dark suits, formal high-level aides nodded in favor or censure as stewards in blue blazers and gray slacks pushed carts of sandwiches into the Cabinet room.

Passing the roped-off Oval Office Linda paused. It was empty. Mesmerized by the soundless power, there seemed to be a brightness illuminating from within. The only sound she heard was a faint ticking, emanating from a massive clock inside. She caught her breath, remembering all those who had governed from where she stood.

"It's impressive isn't it?" a traditionally dressed woman in her sixties said to Linda. It was Rose Zamaria, a lady who'd run a tight ship for the Bush administration and was affectionately nicknamed, "Mother Superior."[63] She handed Linda a bounded stack of papers, then took her on a tour.

The papers were the Ethics Standards for staffers to follow. It opened with: "President Bush is committed to providing the citizens of the United States with an administration whose officials hold themselves to the highest standards of integrity." Under Rose's keen watch, nothing would tarnish this White House. It was the People's House, and everyone inside represented America. It was protocol to endorse appropriate appearance and conduct. For example, if Rose noticed a female staffer's skirt was too short, she'd be sent home to change. It also instructed administrative procedures, like never leaving a confidential document on your desk even if it was concealed in a folder. Secure your documents in the safe before you leave.

"It was strict but for good reason," Linda remembered.

Although on paper she was hired as a floater, in actuality she rarely floated. Instead of covering for lunch, Linda served in media relations for over a year where colleagues became friends and unpaid White House interns—the crème de la crème of college students—were invaluable assets. "Media relations were so busy, there were never enough hours in the day. We'd be lost without them," Linda reminisced.

So deeply entrenched in the work, the people, and the mission, Linda forgot about floating. In short order, she was earning a stellar reputation as a can-do person—when it was time to float again. But before her next assignment, she was offered a full-time position in media relations. With it came a promotion and a title, but it would've stripped her of the civil service status. If she accepted, she'd be dependent upon the political fortunes or misfortunes of President Bush. As much as she wanted to stay, she declined. As a single mom, she couldn't risk unemployment should the administration change. No president fired careerists and filled those slots with politicals—until the Clintons came to Washington.

From media relations Linda sometimes floated to Vice President Dan Quayle's office, or to the East Wing to First Lady Barbara Bush's office.

"She's dignity and approachability combined," Linda complimented the First Lady. But the majority of her days belonged with the president's staff and she loved it; finding herself repeatedly at Chief of Staff Sam Skinner's office, where she supported intelligence briefings, national security briefings, and meetings at the Oval.

———

It was four months before Election Day and the Bush-Quayle reelection campaign was self-destructing. The polls were predicting a landslide win for the Democratic presidential nominee when a call came in to Linda from the Republican National Convention at the Astrodome in Houston, Texas: "Report to the new deputy chief of staff's office with Jim Baker and Bob Zoellich; Sam Skinner is fired. [64]

The young, handsome Arkansas Governor William Jefferson Clinton; his attorney-wife of the Rose Law Firm, Hillary Rodham Clinton; Tennessee Senator Al Gore, Clinton's vice presidential running mate; and his wife, Tipper, were making serious inroads. The nation was ablaze with anticipation. Linda, who revered President Bush, still thought it was exciting that someone in her generation had won the Democratic nomination.

The Clinton-Gore ticket campaigned on a pledge to usher in the hope and change America needed, promising to build a better world.[65] "Vote for us; for the most ethical administration in history," they guaranteed. It was a similar platform, "Change we can believe in," that Illinois Senator Barack Obama used during the 2008 presidential race to defeat Hillary Clinton.[66]

Hillary and President Obama's mentor Saul Alinsky preached, "The basic requirement of change is to recognize the world as it is. We must work with it on its terms if we are to change it to the kind of world we would like it to be."[67]

The 1992 presidential campaign grew ugly—fast. Political advisors James Carville, Paul Begala, and then Clinton Communications Director George Stephanopoulos (now at ABC's *Good Morning America*), assembled a Clinton war room and were on the attack making fun of President Bush's "Bushisms," chastising him for being out of touch after he went to a grocery store and was unfamiliar with the check-out scanner.[68]

"It's the economy, stupid," "Change vs. more of the same," and "War room" became part of the nation's lexicon. The days of respectful exchanges like "My distinguished opponent" or "worthy opponent" between presidential candidates vanished. The polished speaker Bill Clinton claimed to feel America's pain.[69]

"We were winning ugly. Making history," Stephanopoulos recalled.[70] He was right. No candidate before Bill Clinton had won the presidential nomination amassing such negative ratings while chasing off scandals from draft dodging to infidelity.[71]

History repeats itself. In 2008, Barack Obama won the presidency chasing off scandals from his controversial anti-American relationships to his aunt Zeituni Onyango, an illegal alien, who defied a deportation order and lived in public housing.[72]

"President Bush's decision to fire Sam was a necessary evil in this changing political climate," Linda said. James Baker replaced Skinner as chief of staff. Now, she was assigned to Deputy Chief of Staff Bob Zoellick, whose purview included policy such as the North American Free Trade Agreement (NAFTA), West Wing business, plus participating in the twice daily Core Group meetings in Baker's office, strategizing with the Bush-Quayle '92 campaign.

With the new Baker crowd installed, President Bush's mandate remained intact, and extended during his post-presidency, to not publicly speak out against the Clintons.

"We were told not to respond to any negative campaign rhetoric and focus on the issues and policy differences. No personal attacks," Linda recalled.

With the election nearing, she arrived at work around seven and was lucky to leave near midnight, loving her job, but the pace took its toll. Her mom and stepfather became her angels, moving in temporarily to help with her kids, then seventeen and thirteen years old.

Days before the election, the White House was eerie in its stillness. The spotless Oval Office was empty behind the roped-off open door. The power center of Baker's large corner office sat untouched. Seats were available in the typically busy mess, the White House cafeteria. Senior aides had taken to the campaign trail with President Bush.

Inside the West Wing, operating at full speed, Zoellick continued the West Wing workload while remaining in constant contact with Air Force One or President Bush's campaign train, and Linda was swamped.

On Election Day the staffers were ready to drop from exhaustion, but stayed near the televisions as the results dribbled then flooded in. The

Clintons made history, on November 4, 1992, winning 43% of the vote. For the first time in twelve years a Democrat had won the presidency.[73]

"President Bush felt that he let the American people and his staff down. He was wrong. We let him down," Linda said. "I'm sorry the American people couldn't get to know the George Bush I knew. They would've been comforted that he was at the helm guarding their children and steering international and domestic affairs."

President Bush insisted his staff ensure the Clintons received a welcome and quick transition. Later, Linda showed me a copy of a binder she kept from Andrew Card, who in 2001 became President George W. Bush's chief of staff. He had given it to her for her then boss to sign off on.

Dated November 18, 1992, labeled, "The Office of Presidential Transition," inside the binder was a list of the Executive Branch transition contacts for President-elect Clinton's transition team. Card wrote: "We look forward to a smooth and orderly transition. Please know that I stand ready to help with regard to any problems at anytime."[74] The letter was addressed to the Honorable Vernon Jordan. It was this same Jordan, President Obama's future golf buddy and supporter, who, in 1998, made headlines when he secured a job for President Clinton's paramour, Monica Lewinsky, at Revlon.[75]

Some people know as children, instinctively, what they want to do when they grow up; whether their dream is to be a doctor, movie star, teacher, or serve in the military. For Linda, working at the White House was a childhood dream. An avid history buff and a book lover, her interest was kindled when she was about eight years old. While on a family weekend trip to visit relatives, her mother had given young Linda a book to keep her occupied on the drive. It was a slender, green, hard-covered book with illustrations called *Abe Lincoln Gets His Chance.* In her youthful wonder, she thought how exciting it would be to see the White House, maybe work there too. She was awestruck by Lincoln's humble beginnings, his talent to overcome obstacles. Now not only had Linda seen the White House but served inside, and she kept the book. I saw it later at her house, slightly faded in one of her family room bookcases.

Exiting Linda's van after we parked in front of her home on her Cricket Pass driveway in Columbia, Maryland, I glanced up and down the small peaceful cul-de-sac, eyeing the homes and manicured lawns. A neighbor was walking a dog and children played while I tried to envision the Clinton-Lewinsky press mayhem where I stood. Linda must have noticed.

"Amazing isn't it? I don't even have a fence. The press was literally on top of me," she said, as we headed for her front door. Before she opened it, she briefly stopped. "See that van?" she said, pointing to a white one as she swung her screen door open, catching it with her knee. "That belongs to my neighbor. It's not the press. They usually park further down there," gesturing in the opposite direction. Then she put her house key into her front door lock.

"Excuse the mess," Linda apologized when she opened the door to a bunch of boxes. Her dog, Cleo, a friendly golden retriever, jumped "hello," and a couple black cats scampered down the stairs. "I never seem to have enough time for anything these days," she groaned.

Linda's two-story house was cluttered inside. It was far from the "decimated hovel" she had sarcastically described it to be, earlier. But behind the clutter one could see that her house was once a cozy and charming home. Knickknacks and antiques accented with a European influence, once joyfully handpicked and displayed with great care, now sat dusty and neglected on shelves.

In her family room, photographs with family and friends, abundant with laughter were muted; pushed aside, making space for books and legal documents crammed into a built-in bookshelf. The volumes of *The Starr Report* were partly situated on her mantle shelf where a framed mirror hung over the fireplace. A comfortable couch was positioned against the wall under the windows, which would have shown a street view had her blinds been open. On the other side of the couch was a dark wood hutch with a ceramic blue and white bowl in the space beneath it. That's where her now infamous tapes were casually tossed after one side was recorded, because she worried she'd record over the wrong side by mistake. Now it heaved with newspaper clippings and memos. It was incredible how that exposed and fragile bowl was the storage place for the Tripp-Lewinsky tapes. One couldn't help but think that a person who allegedly conspired to take the down President Clinton might have opted for securer storage.

At first glance it looked like her home had changed to a house; a house for storage. It was full of stacked boxes and papers in random heaps. Linda was leery of throwing things out since she believed that the Clintons paid investigators to ransack their adversaries' garbage, hunting for dirt or for whatever could be spun as dirt, and she'd been meaning to get a shredder.

In her family room on the coffee table lay a stack of supportive letters and cards from people from around the country and the world. They were chock-full of well wishes, with checks addressed to her legal defense fund in many. Several donors apologized for not being financially able to send her more money, "You don't deserve this. ... We need more Americans like you, Linda Tripp," and so forth; nearby was another pile loaded with hate-filled, nasty letters.

It was gloomy inside her house, with the window blinds kept closed, day and night. Streaks of sunlight barely escaped down her hallway toward the family room to meet up with the sole uncovered window in her kitchen that allowed the outside world to be seen.

"Trust me," Linda assured me. "My lawyer checked everything out." No one could see inside the kitchen window she said; plus, her lawyer, Joe Murtha, evidently had a police officer friend who periodically drove by to check on her, just in case. And then she asked me if I were hungry. This was a taste of her new "normal."

———

"Joe Murtha, my lawyer, wants to make sure you aren't a Clinton plant," Linda told me, after I sat down in her family room, which accounted for the nervous energy swallowing her up, while she fed her pets, checked her messages, and straightened out stuff on the counters, at the same time.

The tone in her voice sounded sheepish but it was also dead serious. It was true. Under her lawyer's orders, she was not to share any "major" details with me until he had met me.

Taken aback, I wasn't sure if I should burst out laughing or weep. Me? A Clinton plant? I've been wrongly labeled things before, heard stories about me that were impossible to be true. *But a Clinton plant?* That was a new one. It seemed oddly funny, then frightening. *Is this for real?*

It was.

"Joe is overly protective of me," she continued. "I hope you don't mind?"

No, I didn't mind. I had nothing to hide. Her lawyer could check me out all he wanted. Actually, the possibility that the Clintons might plant someone near one of their so-called enemies roused my brain in that bone-chilling kind of way.

Was her lawyer wise and me a naïve fool? Would the Clintons fiendishly plant a mole to keep tabs on Linda, to influence her? Nah, the implications were too diabolical, and conspiracy-esque to contemplate. But it was a clever idea if the Clintons had skeletons to hide to keep them out of jail, I suppose. Her lawyer had to be overreacting, I convinced myself at the time.

To allay her suspicions, I handed her my wallet, and showed her my ID. Also, I am Canadian. I can't vote in American elections. I didn't have a dog in this race. I offered up my bags for her to search (she declined), and told her she should call my mom, and any references she wanted. Besides, my beat was never politics. It was Hollywood and true crime. Having no political editor or ties to please, she seemed to relax a teeny bit, even more, after I had a phone conversation with her lawyer, whom I would meet soon.

Chapter 5: Co-presidency

"Do not be deceived: 'Bad company ruins good morals.'"

—1 Corinthians 15:33 (ESV)

I was in the Ratwoman's house—that is, if you agree with the description that Hollywood's once highest paid screenplay maestro Joe Eszterhas, of *Flashdance and Basic Instinct* fame, used to describe Linda in his wildly trashy Clinton impeachment book, *American Rhapsody*.

Eszterhas's publisher, Alfred A. Knopf, who later published Bill Clinton's memoir, *My Life,* promoted his tome as a combination of "comprehensive research with insight, honesty, and astute observation to reveal ultimate truths."[76] Wow. Virtually each mention of Linda reeked with disdain as though Eszterhas used a fanged scalpel for a word processor. In his view, she was a chief villain, flawed Clinton-hater, with no hope of redemption. She was a "creep," a "spook," and "a dumpy, stiffly conservative spy among attractive, sexual young people who had taken over the government."[77]

Ick! I guess I'd better be careful. I was in her house.

Over a decade ago, I'd met Eszterhas in Los Angeles. Back then I was a neophyte writer navigating through Hollywood's sneaky smoke and mirrors. It was dicey. I learned fast how there was almost nothing you could take at face value coming out of there. And, I knew a little something about the wisdom of having insurance to safeguard oneself against powerful people who weren't pleased if you knew stuff about them. Perhaps my klieg light experience tilted my opinion in Linda's favor—rightly or wrongly, but at least honestly, toward believing she might have tape recorded Monica for insurance purposes, unlike the Clinton defenders who saw it as a revolting betrayal of friendship. But if a person has never been pitted against the President of the United States or asked to lie in court for him, who can say they wouldn't have taken similar actions? Now, I'd find out whether Eszterhas's non-fiction reporting was as first-rate as his fiction.

Who was Linda Tripp, really? If you subscribed to her detractors' beliefs, the elite media, authors, pundits, and Clinton surrogates, how did she morph from a single mom, government worker into a badass Republican Ratwoman bent on destroying the Clintons to write a hate-infused, tell-all book to make heaps of cash?

I set out to find out. With Linda at work, at the job she retained under the Pentagon umbrella she described as "looking for work" that reportedly paid her about $100,000, I camped out in her family room, devouring stacks of documentation. I poured through published sources from all sides and the OIC investigations, involving firsthand experiences she had with the Clinton White House. [78] By the time she got back, I had a ton of questions for her. After she checked in with her attorney, Joe Murtha, then we'd talk. Little by little, I was transported back into the Clinton White House.

———

It was January 1993. After twelve years of Republican rule, President George Herbert Walker Bush passed the torch to President William Jefferson Clinton.

Emotions of excitement and nostalgia tugged at Linda's heart, as Fleetwood Mac's bouncy refrain of the Clinton campaign, "Don't Stop Thinking About Tomorrow," reverberated in her thoughts during her icy commute into D.C. Yes, she'd miss the Bush White House, yet she'd known this day would come. She looked forward to the cooler politics the Clintons promised. Having taken an oath and sworn to support the institution of the presidency, she was ready to serve and excited to meet the Clintons.

The air was charged with expectation. Her feet couldn't keep up with her beating heart as she raced to the Correspondence office. No one knew whether the rumors of cutbacks were true. Understandably there'd be changes, she reasoned.

This was Linda's first administration transition. She didn't know what to expect. Mountains of mail overflowing from mail carts were arbitrarily lined up in the corridors. With no system in place yet, the usual orderly flow was a wreck. A fellow careerist explained, "The mail more than quadruples when a new president is inaugurated. All over the world people write offering their congratulations, requests, and resumes."

First to be floated out to the West Wing, Linda's assignment was at National Economic Council Director Robert Rubin's office.

When Rubin, the former economic guru from Goldman Sachs, left his government position, "he took a job at Citigroup where the bank's collapse was averted by the injection of $45 billion in taxpayer bailout cash." Reportedly, he currently "wields enormous influence" in the Obama administration.[79]

Crossing West Executive Avenue to the basement lobby entrance, Linda took two steps at a time, to the second floor to report to Rubin's office. Lining the walls of the OEOB, West Wing, everywhere, Linda noticed photographs of First Lady Hillary Rodham Clinton and President Bill Clinton; Hillary's picture separate from Bill—even hanging where the official portraits of the president and vice president had hung for decades. That was her first clue as to the power base in the Clinton administration.

A madhouse party atmosphere rocked the West Wing. Blurs of new faces carting in boxed files and personal mementos bustled by her. Rowdy, celebratory staffers were high-fiving each another in fraternity-styled cheers. The cheers were subdued by loud, aggravated swearing like, "Would someone f—ing answer the f—ing phone?" because the phones were ringing off the hooks. It was nuts.

Inquiring if there was a problem, Linda was told "some a—holes" gave the direct lines to the press. She called a White House operator, who swiftly changed every number and they shared a laugh.

"Remember to only give out the White House switchboard line or you'll never have peace," she directed the new staffers.

Suddenly viewed as a problem solver, she was recommended to help in the Oval Office. It was a plum opportunity for her to make a knockout impression on America's forty-second president. President Clinton was double-checking her credentials. Soon she'd know if she'd received his nod.

Then, she got it; President Clinton's approval. Taking her place five feet in front of the Oval Office in the epicenter of opposing-party administrations, she witnessed a birth of a new era, and a new chapter in America's history books serving directly for President Bill Clinton.

———

Days flew as Linda and I dove deeper into 1600 Pennsylvania Avenue. When reliving the past, a series of emotions often appear; some may be cathartic or painful, regretful or invigorating. There were topics she wanted to avoid; like Vince Foster and what was it like working for Hillary. She'd cringe and brush me off with phrases such as "she's evil," "intimidating," "a nightmare," and "frightening." And then clam up. It was one thing to say Hillary was evil, but I needed to prove it if it were true. I knew I had to play devil's advocate too. Linda's credibility and her motives had been put under fire. Just because she said so, didn't make it true. I'd need other sources to back her up.

In the 1990s the Clintons denied speculation that Hillary acted as co-president, however, during Hillary's failed 2008 presidential campaign, she claimed it was her White House experience that qualified her to be Commander-in-Chief on day one.[80] Linda saw their co-presidency immediately.

When Linda met President Clinton in the Oval Office, she was impressed. "He was charismatic and mesmerizing. You can't be in his presence and not feel a sense of awe."[81] But oddly when they reached out to shake hands, she wanted to shake loose and pull hers back. *What's wrong with me?* she scolded herself. She couldn't help but think when a lion shows his teeth, he's not always smiling.

Yet, whenever she walked someone into the Oval, they received the president's undivided enduring attention. "You had to like the president," Linda said. "He was casual, laid back, friendly, until Hillary arrived."

Linda was in the Oval organizing President Clinton's personal files when Hillary passed through the hallway that housed the study Lewinsky made famous. As Hillary's footsteps neared, she noticed President Clinton and his aide's postures stiffen, guard-like. Initially, Linda didn't understand why. Seconds after Hillary's arrival, a chill punctured the air, and she was also on guard. She instantly learned an explicitly clear rule: There were two camps in this White House. His and hers, and hers terrified his.

Reportedly, "It was vicious ... People were scared of [Hillary] because they knew she could chop off their testicles if she so chose. You did not cross Hillary."[82]

Former Counselor to the President David Gergen also recalled the tension, "With a dozen or so of her husband's aides gathered around, Hillary would let loose a tirade. She'd 'launch a deadly missile straight at [Bill's] heart and just before it hit, the missile would explode, the shrapnel hitting the staff.'"[83]

"Hillary's smile was as electrifying as her husband's," Linda recalled. "She was impressive, a very strong woman, but she was different." Linda couldn't shake this feeling, *something isn't right.* Hillary was more like barbed wire; if you got too close you might get cut. "There's coldness to her embrace, like dead ice," she said.

"Sometimes it was awkward being around the president," Linda recalled, finding herself regularly embarrassed as he kept giving the eye to women in front of Hillary and Hillary didn't care. "No woman was immune to Clinton's roving eye except Hillary's staff; his personal secretary, Betty Currie; and Secretary of State Madeline Albright."

So began Linda's strange foray into the inside joke from Arkansas that became America's first family. Aside from Bill's philandering rumors, which surfaced during the 1992 presidential campaign that culminated in Bill's "I caused pain in my marriage" admission on CBS's *60 Minutes*,[84] Linda couldn't know about the Clintons' history of using staff (like Betsey Wright, former security chief Buddy Young, and then White House staffers) to squash, uh, "bimbo eruptions."[85]

Nor could she have known that Hillary's battle cry defense to crush tawdry allegations about her husband was to always blame and attack political enemies instead of dealing with her husband's issues. Nor could Linda have known how Hillary enlisted private detectives, her alleged "secret police," to discredit anyone who jeopardized their political aspirations.[86]

The first week outside the Oval, an urgent memo addressed to John Podesta, staff secretary, landed on Linda's desk. Whisking it to his office she was struck by an oddity. The urgent memo was from pollsters detailing the polling results on every issue that got President Clinton elected. She was stunned by the pollster's heavy hand in governing.

In 2009, John Podesta, President and CEO of the Center for American Progress, a progressive think-tank funded in part by billionaire open society advocate George Soros, served as co-chair of President-elect Obama's transition team. He currently serves as an "expert consultant" to Hillary's State Department advising on foreign policy priorities.[87]

Running the gamut from gays in the military to abortion; the memo documented which positions to take, what to push, and what to pull back on. It appeared to be a follow-up to ensure President Clinton's re-election in 1996, except it was 1993, and they'd barely unpacked. Linda quickly saw the cooler style of the Clinton White House leadership meant watching President Clinton tend to each decision using polling results—with the First Lady's final seal of approval or rejection. That was the first of a gusher of urgent poll memos she'd rush to a senior advisor or to the president. The Clintons took polls to see where they should go on vacation, and to determine how to react to terrorists' attacks against Americans.[88]

During the 1992 campaign, then Governor Clinton pledged to cut White House Staff by 25 percent.[89] The Clintons kept their campaign promise—initially. Maureen Hudson, with political appointee Marsha Scott (a drop-dead gorgeous woman, former interior decorator, and daughter of Miss Arkansas 1945 and Clyde "Smackover" Scott), were ordered to handle the cuts starting with the correspondence unit—where Linda served.

History dictated that the correspondence unit was a critical lifeline, the institutional backbone for the White House to function. Firing careerists was such a rough assignment for Hudson that she put herself on the top of the list. "She'd rather resign than fire one careerist," Linda said.

Linda loved her job and didn't want to lose it. She kept her head down, worked late making herself indispensable. She wanted to prove to the Clintons she was up for any challenge. Around her, fellow careerists were ordered to pack up and "Get the f–k out" in "an unnecessarily rude, plain mean, gloating, and vindictive manner."

Within a couple weeks the correspondence unit was decimated, transformed into a graveyard of empty desks, turned-over chairs, and knocked-over trash bins.

With tears in her eyes, Linda helped her colleagues carry boxes out as they made their final march down the once-pristine West Wing. Now it looked like a dumpster. Passing half-unpacked boxes cluttering the hall-ways, they walked on coffee-stained carpets, out to the front gate where her fired colleagues turned in their blue passes to the Secret Service. It didn't make sense. As the careerists left, two and then four and then six more politicals arrived, wearing temporary orange passes. The Clintons cancelled out their pledge. They got rid of 25 percent on the career side and increased political hires.[90]

Their edict was clear: no outsiders allowed. Job security would ever-more elude her as she learned the next Clinton rule: them versus us. *Why do the Clintons distrust us so?* she contemplated, troubled. "If you weren't one of them, your days were numbered," she said.

What Linda didn't know at the time was Hillary's decisions were inten-tional. Citing advice from former President Jimmy Carter's wife, Rosalyn, Hillary insisted on "'getting their own people on board' because too many leftovers can cause [the Clintons] problems."[91]

———

It was February 17, 1993, when the West Wing was abuzz preparing for President Clinton's first State of the Union address highlighting the economy. Typically, speechwriters spent weeks preparing and days writing; consulting with senior advisors on policy. Each draft is then sent to the president for editing and approval.

But this was the Clinton White House and what wasn't typical was Hillary. Taking up residency in the Roosevelt Room, Hillary, surrounded by the president's speechwriters and top political operatives, edited and added her policies to the address—without the president. Sitting outside, Linda heard the turmoil, but resisted commenting although a First Lady under the law has *no policy jurisdiction.* Obviously, Hillary knew what she was doing, Linda reasoned.

Before lunch President Clinton handed Linda his edits of the address, "Please make sure the speechwriters get these," he said, before returning to the Oval. Knowing the speechwriters were sequestered with Hillary, Linda went to the Roosevelt Room and knocked on the door border. Feeling the now normal tension, all eyes shifted to her. "I'm sorry to interrupt you, but the president asked me to give you this." Hillary stood and snatched the paper from her hand. Shaking her head as she read it, "No f—ing way are we using any of this s–t," she bristled. [92]

Stunned, Linda's heart free-fell down her chest, "But, but these are the president's personal edits...." Anger raced up Hillary's face, "I don't give a f–k whose edits they are. They are not going in."

By then Linda was used to hearing the word "f–k" from Bill and Hillary and their staffers like "ricocheting bullets used in every conceivable form of speech," but she didn't expect Hillary's toxic reaction to the president's edits. With her head low, Linda deferentially said, "Yes, ma'am," quickly excusing herself, intimidated by the First Lady who ran the place.

A former Clinton speechwriter recalled, "The morning of the [State of the Union] speech, Mrs. Clinton said, 'This is just not good enough,' and sat down in the Roosevelt Room ... with a whole bunch of aides, and worked through the speech paragraph by paragraph."[93]

Later that evening when Linda left for home, she saw the Clintons hunched over a staffer from Arkansas (who was furiously typing), fighting over whose policy would make it into the speech.

"The staff in Arkansas had become accustomed to Bill and Hillary's fierce arguing, but their Washington advisers found it 'demoralizing,'" David Gergen confirmed. "The most unnerving aspect of the Clintons' altercations was their use of profanity, especially 'f–k' and 's–t'—particularly shocking in Hillary's case because of her slightly pious air."[94]

Unsettled by the Clintons' tantrums, Linda, a Christian, found herself many a night leaving the White House to go home and she prayed.

Until Linda was twelve, she was convinced she'd go to hell if she ate bologna on Fridays. Her Italian grandmother was extremely religious. Although Linda drifted from the church, she said she never drifted far from her faith in God. "I never believed that one denomination was better than another, nor do I have to be in church for my prayers to be heard. But I needed guidance. 'Please God, why am I so upset?'"

That night when she watched the State of the Union address, it was clear Hillary had won. "After the First Lady and the many good people ... complete their work, I will deliver to Congress a comprehensive plan for health care reform," President Clinton said.[95]

Linda couldn't help but wonder if only the nation knew how true Bill's "two-for-one" statement on the presidential campaign really was. The

First Lady, an unelected spouse, was illegally writing policy, bypassing the American people and Congress.

History repeats itself. The Obama administration bypassed the American people and Congress by providing a backdoor amnesty to illegal aliens by memo, including to Obama's uncle.[96]

Linda's grim assessment of the Clintons' power shift within their marriage shaped early. When Bill behaved, he had the power; "If he misbehaved, the power shifted to Hillary, the unelected co-president, to govern."

David Gergen concurred, "My sense has been they are on a see-saw in their relationship. ... When she goes up and he goes down, or he goes up and she goes down, there, the balance gets out of whack. ... On health care ... that Troopergate story put that see-saw up so that she went way up. ... And I never saw him challenge her on health care. ... It was very much like watching a golden retriever that has pooped on the rug and just curls up and keeps his head down."[97]

But back in 1993 Linda beat herself up, thinking she should be less judgmental and just relax. Serving at the White House was an honor and privilege. The trick was to not make eye contact with President Clinton and keep a sizeable distance from Hillary. She was honored to serve.

On the national security front, less than ten days later on February 26, 1993, New York City's World Trade Center was bombed by al-Qaeda terrorists, leaving six dead and injuring over one thousand people. An eyewitness said, "It felt like an airplane hit the building."[98] The Clintons didn't bother to visit the site.

Chapter 6: Legal Eagles

"For the love of money is a root of all *kinds of* evil, for
which some have strayed from the faith in their greediness,
and pierced themselves through with many sorrows."

—1 Timothy 6:10 (NKJV)

Near the three-month anniversary of the Clinton administration, Deputy Counsel Vincent Foster, one of Hillary's closest Rose Law Firm colleagues and long-time Arkansas friend, rang Linda's line outside of the Oval Office and asked her to join the Office of Counsel to the President as an executive assistant to Bernie Nussbaum.[99] "No, no, it's not secretarial," the tall handsome Foster said. Nussbaum had a secretary; Foster had a secretary. Linda was not hired to be a secretary.

She had been on loan from the Oval in the counsel's office when she first met Foster. "He seemed so ill-placed in this administration. His kindness and decency and his professionalism made him seem more suited to what I had come to know in the Bush White House."[100]

Style and appearance-wise, Foster was the opposite of Bernie Nussbaun, Counsel to the President. Nussbaum was shorter and balding. He was a brass-knuckled, blunt-spoken, highly regarded New York litigator.

"They were immensely likable in their individual ways," Linda said. Like Foster, Nussbaum shared a long history with Hillary that went back to President Richard Nixon's Watergate investigation where he with Hillary, then an ingénue lawyer, led the effort to impeach President Richard Nixon.[101]

As Linda viewed it, this was Hillary's chance to be reunited with her mentor and ally. In essence, "Nussbaum owed her, and now she had a pair of eyes and willing hands in the West Wing," she said.

Linda should've felt honored to be requested; instead she was amazed. At last, she cautiously began to feel like an accepted part of the Clinton team. Hesitating, she procrastinated because working in the counsel's office seemed to be an unwelcome prospect. Serving in the Bush administration taught her she'd be bogged down with stuffy legal briefs, working on tasks for which she had no experience, like endless judicial nominees, and constitutional laws. Why leave the exciting Oval Office? "What would I be doing exactly?" she asked him.

Despite her reservations, it was Foster who sealed her decision. With his Southern hospitality and a quiet demeanor, his warmth and sincerity made it impossible for her to say no. Although on paper Linda as a floater belonged to the correspondence unit, Hillary's lawyers arranged it for her to permanently work in the counsel's office, and retain her apolitical status should the political winds blow poorly for Nussbaum. Honored to serve, she accepted the offer and plunged in.

If Linda wanted to be where the action was, Hillary's lawyers had given her a ticket. Within days, she was buried in scandals. The damage control started immediately when highly publicized but poorly vetted Clinton White House appointments from the Supreme Court to Attorney General to Secretary of Defense blew up.

According to Bernie Nussbaum's job and title description on paper, Linda's new boss also served as President Clinton's assistant. As a rule, his position ensured a direct line of communication to the president but she noticed at the Oval that Nussbaum's dealings with President Clinton were more ceremonial. A nomination triggered a phone call and more calls as nominees fell apart, but otherwise it was Hillary's show as her nominee choices skidded from whom was the best qualified to whom can we get through? Zoe Baird's and Kimba Wood's Attorney General nominations imploded after it was revealed they had employed illegal aliens.[102] Hillary's final choice, Janet Reno, ultimately was filled. One of Reno's first acts as Attorney General was firing 93 U.S. Attorneys and replacing them with Clinton political appointees.[103]

Quickly, Linda saw that the Hillary-controlled presidential counsel's office, located within two footsteps from her West Wing office, was the hub in the Clinton White House, not the Oval Office. Instead of learning legal issues, she learned more about public relations from the Clintons' counsel's office than from the Bush administration's media relations office.

"Legal issues? What legal issues? It was perpetual damage control, spin, and secret meetings with Hillary and her lawyers," Linda described the counsel's office.

A few short weeks later, Linda craved the mundane she thought the counsel's office represented. It was never to be.

One morning when she arrived at work, sitting on everyone's West Wing desk was a single pink rose, beautifully wrapped in a silk ribbon attached to a delicate card. Inside the envelope, inscribed in calligraphy, was a simple touching note marking the one hundred-day anniversary of the Clinton administration that thanked each staffer for their contribution. Signed, Bill and Hillary.

And then there was Whitewater.

When questions over the Clintons' Whitewater Development Company, Inc., became news on the 1992 campaign trail, the Clintons claimed Whitewater (a parcel of land they purchased in 1978 in Arkansas to develop vacation homes with Jim and Susan McDougal, when Bill was Attorney General) was simply a $68,000 money-losing venture. The controversy faded until the press began poking around at "the relationship between the Clintons," and "the banking activity at two McDougal-controlled financial institutions—Madison Bank & Trust and Madison Guaranty Savings & Loan Association,"—and Hillary's legal counsel role with the Rose Law Firm. In 1986 Madison Guaranty failed, costing U.S. taxpayers $73 million to bail out.[104] Eventually, both McDougals were convicted of fraud.[105]

Another presidential hopeful in another shady land deal. In 2008, then Senator Obama's sweetheart land deal with Tony Rezko drew questions when it was revealed that Obama paid "$300,000 under the asking price" for his Chicago mansion and purchased a strip of the adjacent land from Rezko. Rezko, a Chicago political fixer, who bankrolled Obama's political career, was under a federal corruption investigation.[106] Shortly thereafter, he was found guilty of fraud and money laundering.[107]

There came a time when Linda, as a bona fide member of the Clinton White House counsel's office, was adapting to the Clintons' ways. Her belief in the sanctity of the presidency was enough motivation for her to energetically defend them against what she initially believed (Hillary's battle cry) were political enemies out to get them.

Publicly, the Clinton White House claimed Whitewater was a "blip" on their radar screen, however, behind the scenes it caused more than a minor kerfuffle. With tidal wave force, it swallowed up the press communication office, Hillary's office (all three), and the counsel's office, because Hillary refused to cooperate. As Linda recalled, instead of full-disclosure, she dug in and demanded the staff's loyalty in her brawl. It was brutal.

As George Stephanopoulos remembered Hillary saying in his excellent page-turning book, *All Too Human: A Political Education*, "I want us to fight ... I want a campaign now. ... If you don't believe in us, you should just leave." [108]

"There was always a sense from the beginning that you were either with them or against them," Linda often said. "The notion that you could be just a civil servant supporting the institution was not an option."

Meanwhile Whitewater solidified the obvious and unspoken state of affairs in the Clinton White House, which was the odd division of labor. It was a topic Linda said she was never allowed to discuss with prosecutors when she testified in the Whitewater investigations.

Foster and his assistant, Deb Gorham, handled the Clintons' personal and private matters—not America's business. They were consumed with the Clintons' tax returns, their personal legal issues, and Whitewater. Linda remembered how Gorham was run ragged between her desk, Hillary's office, and Foster's desk, which might explain why in June 1993 Foster filed three-years of delinquent Whitewater corporate tax returns. [109] While Linda's boss, Nussbaum, testified that Whitewater wasn't "on the radar screen," it was on Foster's, who called Whitewater "a can of worms you shouldn't open." [110]

And it was. After Congressional pressure in 1995, the Clinton White House, after stalling for months, begrudgingly, released some Whitewater documents that included a handwritten note from Foster. It showed he was concerned about an IRS audit beginning if the Clintons declared losses on Whitewater. He also noted that "it was not possible for the Clintons to substantiate claims they made during the campaign—and after." [111]

Concerned, one afternoon, Linda, went to her boss, "Why is it that Vince acts as the Clintons' personal attorney? In the Bush White House the counsels worked to support the institution of the presidency, and never had enough hours in the day to do it."

"This isn't the Bush White house. Vince represented them in Little Rock and will continue in that role here," Nussbaum answered, ending the conversation.

Linda naïvely hoped this division was temporary; it wasn't. Until the day Foster died his hand rarely touched issues affecting the institution of the presidency.

"He appeared to try," Linda recalled, "like during the nominee vetting process. But every time, other, more pressing issues concerning his true client, Hillary, stole him away from his real job." Referring to Hillary as "the client," Foster's dismay grew with her "callous accelerated disdain, her irritation, and anger directed at the staffers over dealing with her White-water personal problems." Linda shuddered. It crushed and chipped away at Foster, at all of them.

––––––

It was well past 9:30 p.m. when a knock thumped on Linda's door. Behind it stood the man I'd heard so much about, her criminal lawyer, Joseph Murtha. He was stopping by to meet me, and I guess to double check that I wasn't a Clinton plant. "I told you," Linda said, "Joe's a workaholic. I'd be lost without him."

Smaller in stature than I originally envisioned, with brown hair, a wrinkled suit, and a choir-boy face, Murtha shook my hand, sizing me up, friendly style. He sidestepped over the scattered boxes in Linda's hallway to get to the family room. Taking a seat across from me, Murtha eased back comfortably in a winged chair, "Don't worry. I'm used to the mess by now."

At the time Murtha was a partner with the Baltimore law firm of Irwin Green & Dexter, specializing in criminal litigation in both state and federal courts. According to his bio, "Mr. Murtha's significant talent and career accomplishments have been featured in several feature news stories and profiles."[112]

Initially brought in as Linda's co-counsel shortly after the Clinton-Lewinsky scandal broke, Murtha, a Democrat, was her lead counsel. He was also in charge of her legal defense fund which paid his fees.

Prior to working at the Clinton White House, Linda never had a lawyer. She handled her own divorce. After the Clinton-Lewinsky scandal broke,

Linda was notified that her divorce decree had been unearthed, and was released in the press. "I was told that an Assistant Director of Communications at the White House got them," she said. "It was an invasion, but also must have been pretty dull reading."

Linda's history of needing lawyers began when she was first subpoenaed in the Clinton Whitewater investigations where she received what she described as a White House-appointed lawyer, Kirby Behre. Two other lawyers replaced Behre after she fired him, during the frantic early days prior to the Clinton-Lewinsky scandal breaking. The first lawyer, who apparently had Republican-leaning views, didn't stay long. He was fired when Linda was convinced his political agenda and his advice did not reflect her best interests. To her costly regret, by following his counsel, she waived her Fifth Amendment rights when she accepted federal immunity from Ken Starr's OIC in the Lewinsky-Clinton investigation.

The second lawyer was a workers comp attorney, who brought in his childhood friend, Joe Murtha. Now only Murtha and her civil lawyers remained.

"I don't know how I would've survived without Joe," Linda smiled, relaxed by his arrival. "He's the one person I know I can count on. I trust him with my life."

After probing me with rounds of questions, until (I presumed) he was satisfied that I wasn't a Clinton plant, Murtha leaned forward to discuss the latest phase of Linda's criminal case. Cloaked in an aura of expertise, he clenched his hands and appeared to be choosing his words carefully, while he explained absolutely nothing. Rather, he spoke in revolving door-like phrases, such as, "It's very complicated …," "endless battles …," "the Clinton administration will stop at nothing …," accompanied by long sighs.

"I may be a Democrat, but this is wrong," Murtha declared. "I'll fight until the bitter end to ensure Linda has justice."

She loved it that her lawyer was a Democrat. "It's not about politics for him. It's about right and wrong," she said.

"Oh, yes," Murtha affirmed. "This is a case of a lifetime because of the injustice. It's the right thing to do. I've got to look out for Linda. She's not just my client but a friend," he mused. She beamed.

I tried asking them some questions—*tried* being the operative word.

On the topic of Ken Starr and the OIC, for instance, I asked whether or not Starr was helping her regarding the Maryland criminal charges. Linda began answering affirmatively when Murtha abruptly cut her off, finishing her sentence for her. He sternly insisted that this information was not for public consumption and reverted to his swivel, "It's so complicated … endless battles …," chatter. Perhaps my taken aback expression prompted him to soften up when he added how he would explain everything later; adding that he would "facilitate" in any way possible.

I listened to him for a while, then said, "Isn't it important for people to know that Starr was going to bat for her—" when Linda opened her mouth to speak and Murtha cut her off again. Then something unsaid seemed to pass between them. I tried a few more easy questions, like, "What did you think of Ken Starr when you first met him?" When Linda managed to say, "He's a professional who was trying to do his job. But I worried that he may not have realized the corruption he faced with the Clintons—" before Murtha cut her off, this time firing a "hush-up" look her way. She obeyed. That was hardly what I expected from the so-called evil Linda Tripp who allegedly had the nerve to conspire to destroy President Clinton. It was strange, the only person Murtha would discuss without a censor was Monica Lewinsky—negatively.

But there was more misinformation, I'd encounter. Technically, and I guess in Hillary's opinion, I'd crossed over the threshold of the vast right-wing conspiracy. There I was with the alleged ringleader and chief Clinton-hater who, as the story goes, had conspired with the Clintons' political enemies and worked with the sex-crazed, right-wing zealot prosecutor Ken Starr to subvert the American justice system in an effort to destroy the Clinton administration. I was in the perfect spot to stumble upon whatever the VRWC was plotting next to finish the job of destroying the Clintons. But instead this is what I found: nothing.

Never once over the course of several months did I see anyone from Hillary's vast right-wing conspiracy, or one Republican stop by to visit Linda. Nor had one of them telephoned her to see how she was doing or to see what else she might have on the Clintons. Instead, aside from her lawyer, her friend Kim, and her fantastic, supportive, and patriot family (whom I was fortunate to meet later), I saw that she was alone.

And now this; a lawyer calling the shots and censoring her regarding *harmless* information that was positive for Linda and for Ken Starr—who was also vilified by the Clintons and the mainstream press.

History repeats itself. In 2011, liberal groups, including a Hillary associate, launched an "anti-Darrell Issa crusade" to discredit the House Oversight and Government Reform committee chairman. Issa, like Ken Starr, who was tasked to investigate the Clinton White House, is tasked to investigate the Obama White House.[113]

After a few more dodges, "It's complicated … endless battles" revolving stonewalls, he flashed us a church smile and stood up with an exaggerated stretch, "It's getting late. Linda, I'll call you in the morning," he said.

After swapping schedules, mine was open, flexible; Murtha would have to get back to me; with much ballyhoo, he promised to soon provide me with all the information about the vast right-wing conspiracy, the OIC, and the documentation that would vindicate his client and expose the Clintons. Initially, I viewed Linda's attorney as another silver tongued money-grubbing lawyer out for himself, but over time, I started suspecting much worse. He was taking orders and protecting someone else, and it wasn't Linda Tripp. The deeper I got into the Clinton White House with Linda, the more I learned the strategies and tactics the Clinton White House used to stay in power while chasing off investigations, and after having more censoring dealings with Murtha, it occurred to me that his stonewalling and controlling cageyness reminded me of the lawyers Linda would so vividly describe who had served in the Clinton White House. Come, take a look.

Chapter 7: Tow-the-Line

"So when you, a mere human being, pass judgment on them and yet do the same things, do you think you will escape God's judgment?"

—Romans 2:3 (NIV)

Maureen Hudson was guiding Linda through a corridor, passing offices where Theodore and Franklin Roosevelt once worked, when they stopped at a two-suite office for one of Linda's first floats, in the Bush I White House in 1991. "You'll really like it here," Maureen told her. "Several of the staffers have been here for over twenty-five years."

Inside, the phones rang non-stop and faxes were flying out of the fax machine. At one end of the room, a burly fifty-something, salt-and-pepper-haired man stood with a courier as he signed for a package while cradling the phone on his shoulder. Spotting Hudson, he waved hello.

"That's not a problem," Linda could overhear him say as they neared him, "Change all forty-six people. Correct? No, no need to apologize. Yes, sir. All the visas cleared. Tell the president to consider it done. I'll have the revised itinerary by 5:00 p.m. Have a safe trip."

Hanging up the phone, the man smiled warmly. "We're really glad to have you with us," he said to Linda, as he held out his hand, and shook hers firmly. "I'm Billy Dale. Welcome to the travel office."

The White House travel office was the president's private travel agency and Linda's first experience with career staff, outside of the correspondence unit. Travel Director Billy Dale served eight presidents during his thirty-one year career. "The people at travel were amazing," Linda said. "They worked hard, were apolitical. They were there to serve each incumbent and happy to do it."

Linda with ease recalled Dale's pride and honor to serve. "He effortlessly coordinated complex itineraries." It was his efficiency in times of crisis that really impressed her. "This wasn't a job, but a career for Billy and his staff," Linda raved. "All I did was watch in amazement and awe at how they worked."

Instantly her tone plunged. It was as if I'd been flung to May 19, 1993, to the travel office firings; to what became the first Clinton scandal: Travelgate.

"Billy Dale was escorted out of the White House by the FBI, put into a paneled van with no seats and told to sit on the floor the day the Clintons removed him," Linda vividly recalled. "And I watched Hillary orchestrate that whole thing; siccing the FBI on them, getting them out," she fumed. "Careerists, while they're not political, do serve at the pleasure of the president. All President Clinton had to say was, 'We're replacing you.' It would've been unheard of, but was within his legal purview to do." Instead the Clintons did what Linda said they always did: "Destroy their enemy and ruin them."

The abrupt travel office firings were triggered by what the Clinton White House claimed were allegations of sloppy accounting. In December 1994, Billy Dale was indicted on two counts of embezzlement.[114] The press went berserk criticizing the new administration.

In its aftermath, five of the staffers were reinstated, and in a self-critical report the White House admitted it "erred and would never again short-circuit proper legal channels by bypassing the Justice Department in seeking an FBI investigation."[115]

Hillary described Travelgate with cool indifference as, "perhaps worthy of a two-or-three-week life span, instead, in a partisan political climate, it became the first manifestation of an obsession for investigation that persisted into the millennium."[116] But for Billy Dale, it wasn't a partisan manifestation. It was the termination of a thirty-plus-year career, and a fight for his freedom. If convicted, he faced a maximum of twenty years in prison and up to $500,000 in fines.[117]

Saul Alinsky's first rule on the ethics of means and ends was "that one's concern with the ethics of means and ends varies inversely with one's personal interest in the issue. ... 'We all have strength enough to endure the misfortunes of others.'"[118]

Draped in a wider tale of corruption, after the firings, it was widely speculated that the Clintons' friends were vying for the travel office business—an allegation Linda agreed with. She knew, she said, because she floated to the travel office under both the Bush I and the Clinton administrations.

It was the end of January 1993 when Linda met a bubbly blond outside the West Executive wing of the White House compound. The woman introduced herself as Catherine Cornelius, one of Bill Clinton's distant cousins. Cornelius worked for David Watkins, the assistant to the president in management and administration, and handled the Clintons' 1992 presidential campaign travel arrangements with World Wide Travel. Not recognizing Linda from the campaign, Cornelius asked her where she worked.

A couple days later Linda's phone rang outside the Oval Office. It was Cornelius asking if she could float to the travel office to cover so she and a colleague could celebrate World Wide Travel's new business venture with the Democratic National Committee. [119]

Linda could do it only if her desk was covered and sometimes she could. At the travel office she met long-time Clinton friend from Arkansas, the Emmy Award-winning producer of *Designing Woman*, Harry Thomason. Thomason, who produced Clinton's 1992 campaign film, *A Boy from Hope*, was part owner of the air-charter consultant firm TRM Inc. TRM Inc. teamed up with World Wide Travel to handle the 1992 campaign travel arrangements.

During the Clinton-Lewinsky investigation, the press accused Linda of inserting herself into the Clinton scandals. It was a perception which became a false reality. As she explained, "Floaters don't choose where they work; we are told where to go. I did not create the scandals. I was placed in close proximity to where the scandals were taking place."

Instead, Linda felt more like Forest Gump. When she wasn't in the travel office, she was outside the Oval, where she'd see Thomason meet with President Clinton. Then, when she was transferred to the counsel's office, there was Thomason again; this time, meeting with Hillary or one of her associates.

Linda claimed overhearing Thomason conferring with David Watkins where they planned the travel office's demise. "They must've thought I was a piece of furniture," she said to me. Thomason was spreading false corruption rumors to cash in on the travel business. Dale and his colleagues had to go. A pretext for the firings was created, and the trigger was pulled. Thomason, in his defense, said he told, "the White House about what [he] thought was an outrageous practice ... where an office in the U.S. government would not ... talk to businesses about doing business with them."[120]

It was at the counsel's office where the final decision to fire the travel office occurred. Linda knew, she said, because she worked for Bernie Nussbaum at the time.

Using public sources and official reports, combined with Linda's memory, following is a partial chain of events leading up to the travel office firings.

- May 12, 1993: Thomason meets with President Clinton for fifteen minutes, then with Foster, and then with Hillary. Thomason then meets with Watkins, Cornelius, and Foster to discuss the corruption rumors. Counsel Bill Kennedy, Hillary's former law partner at the Rose Law firm, joins in. Foster to Kennedy: "Hillary wants us to contact the FBI and initiate an investigation of the travel office." Hillary's order was a violation of government guidelines, which prohibits the White House from initiating low-level contacts with the FBI—*to avoid political abuse.*[121] Overwrought, Linda felt like she was caught in Watergate. (Ultimately Bill Kennedy was reprimanded for his role in Travelgate and forced to resign after concealing his failure to pay nanny taxes.[122])
- May 13: Thomason meets with President Clinton and Hillary in Foster's office with Chief of Staff Thomas Franklin "Mack" McLarty, a lifelong friend of Bill Clinton from Arkansas, a progressive Democrat and Obama supporter.[123] Hillary says, "What the f–k is being done with the travel office?" Kennedy calls the FBI: "We need an answer now. If you don't do anything, I'm calling the IRS. The highest levels of the White House are interested." [124]
- The White House starts drafting talking points anticipating firing the travel office staff that day. FBI agents arrive at the counsel's office determining there are insufficient grounds to warrant an FBI investigation.[125] The agents' decision changes after Cornelius shares the kickback rumors she'd gotten from Thomason.[126]
- Meanwhile, the day before, Foster and Watkins devise a plan to conceal the improper contact with the FBI by conducting a quickie

travel office financial audit using the accounting firm Peat Marwick to serve as an after-the-fact basis for calling the Feds to justify the firings.

- May 14: Thomason and Cornelius meet with McLarty in the morning and urge him to fire the travel office employees that day. Foster intervenes, "Hold on, we haven't conducted the financial audit yet." McLarty agrees. Hillary doesn't. Watkins also supports Foster's audit cover-up plan but his notes show worry: "What are negative consequences if NO criminal violations. ... FBI would not ordinarily get involved." Hillary is impatient and tells Foster to have Watkins contact her where she repeats her demands for "immediate action."[127]

- May 15-16 (weekend): The audit turns up no evidence of kickbacks. Hillary continues to pressure McLarty to fire the travel office. [128]

- May 17: McLarty succumbs to Hillary's pressure and tells Watkins that Hillary wants "immediate action." Watkins later writes to McLarty, "We both knew that there would be hell to pay if we failed to take swift and decisive action in conformity with the First Lady's wishes."[129]

- May 19: Watkins fires five of the seven travel office employees. The other two staffers, who are out of the country, learn of their dismissals from news reports. Director of White House Security, Craig Livingston, a former bouncer from Arkansas, secures the office. Watkins gives Press Secretary Dee Dee Myers talking points falsely describing the dismissals as the result of a routine review and notes the White House contact with the FBI.[130]

In the counsel's office, everyone was in a panic. Foster knew this was false. He frantically tried to contact Watkins to remove any FBI mention but it was too late because Press Secretary Myers announced it in her normal press briefing. It was colossal damage-control time at the Clinton White House.

"No one dared defy Hillary," Linda re-stated, and that included the president and the ranks. Hillary's associates closed in to protect the Clintons' role in the firings. It got much worse for Vince because he always had to clean up Hillary's messes. (Foster would spend some of the last days before his death looking for a personal attorney.)[131]

How was the clean-up and damage control to protect the Clintons accomplished? By working on what Hillary called their "cohesive strategy," Linda recalled, describing it as what Americans would hear, regardless of the truth. "In every investigation we were told exactly what happened and what to say, and suddenly that became the so-called truth."

Stephanopoulos cited the "cohesive group's" public relations role like this: "What were the Clintons going to say—and how were they going to say it?"[132]

It was in Hillary's counsel's office, where Linda explained how she learned the Clintons' public relations strategy on how to deal with the press regarding Whitewater, Travelgate—all the subsequent investigations. In addition to the "cohesive strategy," a "well-practiced proven formula" called the Three Talking Points was used. "These were statements determined by the polls that would answer all questions no matter what the question was," Linda recounted. "Nobody from the White House spoke to the press core unless their three points were burned into their psyche because one wrong answer, a minor slip, could lead to another explosion."

In murder-board style, Linda described how she sometimes played reporter firing the "spokesperson" with hard and off-topic questions, until any subject asked by the press was swiftly redirected and answered with the Clintons' agenda.

According to Linda, the Clintons' main talking points focused on these themes:

1. Move on, we're above the fray, nothing here.
2. These petty partisan and/or political enemies are mudslinging to derail our agenda, or destroy the Clintons, and the American people know better.
3. We're doing important work for our country.

Saul Alinsky taught, "We repeatedly get caught in this conflict between our professed moral principles and the real reasons why we do things—to wit, our self-interest. We are always able to make those real reasons in words of beneficent goodness—freedom, justice, and so on."[133]

"The press core didn't have a chance," Linda sighed. No matter what frustrated reporters asked about Whitewater or Travelgate, the Three Talking

Points answered all. Even better, they stuck to any quick news overview, a headline, or a sound bite. The longer the investigations dragged on, the more it benefited the Clintons because the public tuned out, only remembering the key talking points, regardless of any inconvenient facts.

The more Linda spoke, the more I saw that the press took whatever they could get as the Clintons Hollywood-ized politics and ultimately the justice system, by controlling what was reported and more importantly, what was not reported in the court of public opinion. Writing a critical article about the Clintons, for example, meant no access for that journalist. Getting access to boost circulation and ratings meant having to play by the Clinton White House rules. That nifty trick was a Hollywood maneuver where publicists deny reporters' access to their celebrity clients unless their clients receive selective and fawning press coverage.

This hard-nose tactic to control the narrative saw daylight during Hillary's failed 2008 presidential bid when *Politico* reported, "Clinton Campaign kills negative story," recounting how *GQ Magazine* was instructed to kill the piece they were writing on the infighting in Hillary's campaign or lose access to Bill Clinton for their "Man of the Year" December issue.[134] *GQ Magazine* caved in and spiked the story.

History repeats itself. In April 2011, Obama White House officials "banished" a *San Francisco Chronicle* reporter who had videotaped protesters interrupting an Obama fundraiser—then claimed they didn't after they were exposed.[135] Shortly thereafter, the regime refused full press access to the *Boston Herald* claiming pool reporters are chosen based on whether they cover the news "fairly," and yelled at a CBS reporter for asking about the "Fast and Furious" gunrunning operation, a Justice Department and Alcohol, Tobacco, Firearms, and Explosives (ATF) operation that allowed Mexican drug cartel intermediaries to purchase guns at licensed U.S. firearms dealers and then cross the border.[136]

President Clinton was first to set the stage for the Travelgate narrative. He wrapped up Travelgate's cohesive strategy ("not my decision ... concerned about sloppy accounting ... we're trying to save money") in a do-good defense. On May 25, he claimed, "I had nothing to do with any decision except to try to save the taxpayers and the press money. The press had been complaining for years that they were overcharged."[137]

However, President Clinton's allegations (and cohesive strategy) are false. The Justice Department failed to prove corruption and no media organizations complained of being overcharged. Meanwhile, the FBI interrogated Billy Dale's daughter, recently back from her honeymoon, demanding to know how her wedding was paid for.

Hillary, publicly and under oath, also denied any direct involvement, echoing the cohesive strategy, "Although I had no decision-making role with regard to the removal of the travel office employees ... I expressed my concern ... that if there were fiscal mismanagement in the travel office ... it should be addressed promptly."[138]

Saul Alinsky's tenth rule of the ethics of means and ends "is that you do what you can with what you have and clothe it with moral garments."[139]

But there was a problem. When a travel office memo written by David Watkins—one similar in tone to others Linda said existed but *weren't* given to investigators, was revealed in the press three years *after* the firings, skeptical eyes turned to Hillary.

The memo read in part: "Once this made it onto the First Lady's agenda, Foster became involved, and he and Harry Thomason regularly informed me of her attention—as well as her insistence that the situation be resolved immediately by replacing the travel office staff." Hillary conveyed "her desire for swift and clear action."[140]

Hillary maintained that her "expression of concern" was misconstrued and "taken to mean something more," washing her hands from responsibility and placing the blame on Watkins and Foster.

Special Prosecutor Robert Ray (who succeeded Ken Starr in the Office of the Independent Counsel), didn't agree with Hillary. Seven years after the firings, he concluded in his final report that Hillary's sworn testimony was "factually inaccurate." "The overwhelming evidence establishes that she played a role in the decision to fire the employees. ... Thus, her statement to the contrary under oath was factually false."[141]

Seven years later, the public had tuned out. Ten years later, the Clintons re-wrote the facts about Travelgate in their respective memoirs absolving Hillary of any wrongdoing or of telling falsehoods to investigators—a prosecutable offense.

Billy Dale didn't believe justice was served. After fighting his criminal charges for almost three years, he was exonerated after a jury deliberated for one hour.[142] After Ray's report was released, Dale said, "Everyone, especially Robert Ray, knows Hillary Clinton lied under oath about her role. It is disappointing that the Office of Independent Counsel ... would not prosecute her simply because of a fear of what a Washington, D.C., jury might do."[143]

I asked Linda why she didn't warn Billy Dale. Conceivably other staffers could have warned him too. She defensively said she wanted to warn him, *tried* to tell the truth but did not because she was terrified of Hillary, of losing her job and her pension. Moreover, she insisted, "It wasn't possible to tell the whole truth afterwards either, not with a White House-appointed attorney breathing down your neck."

"The White House wishes you luck, Linda," she recalled her White House-appointed lawyer telling her, describing how intimidated she felt. "They wanted me to pass along some advice. If you're not 110% sure, it's probably a good idea just to say, 'I can't recall or I have no specific recollection.' And you know you're never to offer any information or speculate. The investigators are just on a fishing expedition."[144]

President Clinton followed that same script. In a deposition during the Paula Jones case, for instance, he testified: "My goal in this deposition was to be truthful, but not particularly helpful. I do not wish to do the work of the Jones lawyers."[145] George Stephanopoulos's lawyer prepped him too: "Remember the ground rules. Tell the truth, but don't say more than you know. If you don't remember what happened, say so. Don't speculate, don't wonder, don't muse, don't imagine—don't try to be helpful."[146]

All good lawyers prepare clients, but there's a difference between prepping and coaching; especially when the coaching hollows-out the truth in favor of the Clintons by controlling and limiting testimony to conceal the truth.

According to Independent Counsel Robert Ray's final report: "Witnesses' lack of cooperation took several forms. Not only were private attorneys ordered to instruct their White House clients not to answer questions based on the Clintons' claim of attorney-client privilege, but the Clinton White House withheld evidence by refusing to provide subpoenaed documents."[147]

This coordinated effort by the Clinton White House is called a "joint defense" or being part of the "joint defense agreement." It became public during the Clinton-Lewinsky investigation where witnesses could not communicate with one another; lawyers, however, may legally share information among others lawyers.[148] As Linda recounted, her attorney had "daily conference calls with the White House to update them."[149]

I was becoming privy to how the Clinton White House dodged (at minimum) a perjury indictment during Travelgate, and seeing the strategies and tactics they used to accomplish that: White House-appointed lawyers, coaching, the joint defense agreement, and the cohesive strategy, which like the Three Talking Points ensured that Americans received the Clintons' agenda of innocence. This was only the beginning.

Linda's employment survival (like other Clinton staffers) depended on the Clintons' survival and an unholy alliance was born. For Linda, what might have begun as a rationalized concession or accommodation to please the president and First Lady would evolve into something far more damaging. Her silence during Travelgate became her sanction. Travelgate was an omen of future events.

There was misery and shame in Linda's voice for her participation. "If the Clintons could trump up charges against Billy," she sniffed. "They could do it to anyone."

It appears that's what happened—to Linda. Six years later she was indicted in an off shoot of another Clinton investigation where Bill was "factually incorrect"—perjured himself.

For Billy Dale, the abrupt travel office firings that led to his criminal indictment came without warning. For Linda, the year-long, off-and-on media speculation beginning the summer of 1998 during the Clinton-Lewinsky investigation (when Linda was called to testify as a federal witness against President Clinton) kept tipping her off. A year later she was indicted for illegal wiretapping in Maryland for recording her phone conversations with Monica Lewinsky.[150]

Five years after the travel office firings, during the Clinton-Lewinsky investigation, Linda tried to explain to the jury: "And I will never forgive myself for not warning [the travel office staff] when I saw what was being done to them. But I didn't. I chose to be loyal to the *Office of the Counsel to the President* [italics mine] for whom I worked and made a decision not to give them fair warning about what was going to happen to them."[151]

Contrary to conventional wisdom that Linda was a whistleblower who conspired to destroy the Clintons, the strange truth was the exact opposite.

Linda *protected* the Clintons. She chose to be loyal to Hillary Clinton to keep her job. It would take courage for her to publicly admit her role in towing the Clinton White House line at the expense of the travel office. But she was ready to come clean, and vindicate them as a warning for others.

Witnessing her life dedicated in large measure to her defense for her trial, one could see it was a stressful time, with little wiggle room for joy. She had to keep on keeping on, working, and living life. But like a boomerang, the indictment always flew back to take her breath away. Although Linda put up a tough front, facing criminal jeopardy was a nightmare. Her main dread was that the Clintons would be able to brand her a convicted felon. "I've never had a speeding ticket. But look, they tried it with Billy. I have to be prepared for the worst."

Billy Dale was wrongly fired from his job. He accrued $500,000 in legal bills (ultimately, Congress voted to pay for all the travel office staffers' legal fees—against President Clinton's angry objections).[152] Dale didn't return to the White House. In contrast, Linda had her $100,000-a-year Pentagon job, was awaiting trial, and her legal bills were financed by legal defense fund donations. When I pointed that out, she balked: "The only reason the Clintons didn't fire me is because of the press attention. But they removed me as a director of a Secretary of Defense program and stuck me in a less visible location, essentially ending my twenty-year career in government. Once they leave office, my job is history."[153]

Chapter 8: The Death of Vince Foster

"Woe to those who call evil good and good evil, who put darkness for light and light for darkness, who put bitter for sweet and sweet for bitter!"

—Isaiah 5:20 (AMP)

"Linda, let's go back to the day Vince Foster died," I said.

That would be July 20, 1993, when White House Deputy Counsel to the President of the United States Vincent Walker Foster Jr. was found dead in Fort Marcy Park. It was the highest-ranking suicide in government since 1949, when President Truman's Secretary of Defense, James Forrestal, committed suicide.[154]

About a month earlier, on the national security front, the FBI had apprehended Omar Abdel Rahman, the Egyptian blind sheik. He received a lifetime in jail for crimes related to the first World Trade Center bombings and other plots. The *9/11 Commission Report* stated, "Neither President Clinton, his principal advisers, the Congress, nor the news media felt prompted, until later, to press the question whether the procedures that put the blind sheik behind bars, would really protect Americans against the new virus of which [he] was just the first symptom."[155] Rahman's arrest foreshadowed the Clinton administration's approach to terrorism: use law enforcement's strong arm to combat it.

For Linda, officially one of the last people to see Foster alive, the sudden death of Hillary's colleague and President Clinton's childhood friend was her first encounter with the idea of suicide. The haunting "why, why, why?"

questions that could never be answered taunted her. "Why did Vince do it? What was so terrible?" she would say to me, giving her troubled thoughts a voice. "Why didn't I see something and stop him, help him?" she cried out at times, still blaming herself.

After Foster died, it was easy for Linda to immerse herself at work, and shove aside the disturbing thoughts that she had somehow failed him; but at night the haunting reflections crept back in. Her mind repeated, *Could I have stopped him?*

In search for peace, answers, anything, she drove to the nearest bookstore, bought everything that dealt with death and suicide, and, like former aide George Stephanopoulos, Linda sought outside help. Stephanopoulos began weekly sessions with a therapist "for all the usual reasons," but the reasons "were magnified by the shock of Foster's suicide."[156] For Linda, no book, no person could explain, nor did the official findings appear to calm her angst. Linda's angst manifested itself in a form you could see: her weight gain that began after Foster died.

When I met Linda in 2000, seven years had passed since his death; and her self-recriminations hadn't faded. Foster's death seemed to eat at her soul, sometimes overwhelming her when I brought it up. Instead of answering my questions—questions prompted by her testimony and public statements—she changed the subject to safer territory; to another gossipy Lewinsky story. Other times, she exclaimed, "I don't know what really happened," or she hid behind her self-constructed wall of rationalizations. "Casting blame won't bring Vince back," she'd insist, "nor is it my place to lay credence to conspiracy theories." Which was true—if the official findings were correct; and it was Linda who implied otherwise during the Lewinsky-Clinton investigation.[157] But what really heightened my suspicions about his death was that we'd gone over the Clintons' "cohesive strategy" and "joint defense" tactics. I knew how they worked. Why did she constantly contradict herself?

"No one challenged Hillary, not low-on-the-totem-pole me all the way up to senior staff and the president," she repeatedly said, clearly still intimidated.

Yet, after all this time, she still heeded their warnings. "What couldn't you tell investigators about Vince's death that you wanted them to know but were too afraid to tell?" I'd ask her.

And she would dodge, sometimes getting angry. "I told you," she bristled, "I was afraid I'd lose my job. I had kids at home, my pension. You don't understand. You don't have kids."

And she was right; but at the same time, I couldn't help but wonder what she could lose now—if there was something to tell. She'd been trashed by the media, threatened, put into a safe house, felt the full force of the Clinton machine, and as a political appointee, was about to lose her job. Her kids, now young adults, had left home; and she was still tight-lipped and defensive. How could I not think she wasn't hiding something?

One afternoon, out of the blue, Linda surprisingly and unnecessarily apologized for her grief over Foster's death. She was afraid it might appear disproportionate, considering the short time she had known Foster (which was not quite six months). She wanted to be clear.

"Vince was not just someone I worked for, but a friend," she said, defending her sorrow. Then she overcompensated by describing how their bond was forged quickly with a shared camaraderie amid their hectic high-pressure jobs in Hillary's counsel's office. Other times she would simply lament, "If only Vince were alive ..." how "Vince would've understood"— referring to her predicament with the Clintons.

"You could trust Vince with anything, such a decent soul," she told me. "I wish you could've met him." Had he lived, Foster would've been the person she would have trusted to help her navigate through the treacherous months of the Clinton-Lewinsky scandal.

"Vince Foster's backyard touched [Bill Clinton's] when he lived with his grandparents in Hope, Arkansas. [Bill and Vince] were friends virtually all their lives."[158] "Foster was one of the best lawyers Hillary had ever known and one of the best friends she'd ever had."[159]

For the Clintons, who had also suffered a loss, his death sparked a firestorm that engulfed the nation. The charges leveled against them were serious: Foster knew too much. *They had killed him.* Clinton staffers removed files from his office. *Must be a cover-up.* Investigators never found the fatal bullet. *It's a conspiracy.* And on and on it went.

Despite five government investigations that concluded Foster committed suicide in Fort Marcy Park, the conspiracy beast was still on the prowl. Were the Foster conspiracy theories viable or were they created by the right for political gain?

Having finished dinner, Linda emerged from the kitchen and sat on the couch across from me. Ahead would be a long night. I spun my chair around to face her. On the table were two large three-ringed black binders. Inside the binders housed what the public knew: copies of White House press briefings and OIC Reports with media articles stacked alongside them. Handing Linda a copy of what I'd reconstructed, I glanced at her, trying to gauge her mood. Would she procrastinate, balk, or change the subject as before? Or would she explain what she meant: why the dishonesty during the Foster investigations had shaken her so? [160]

I relished what I knew would be my short-lived reprieve from Linda's lawyer, Joe Murtha (whom I had since met on several occasions), and his non-stop interruptions and censorship. Thank God, he was at his farm, which he had bought since representing Linda. Could we vindicate the innocent? Expose the guilty if guilt applied? Bring closure and peace to Foster's family? Clear the cloud of suspicion hovering over Bill and Hillary? Was even thinking we could end the controversy a farfetched hope? Frankly, I wondered if anyone could, but I had to try.

Unbeknownst to me, I was about to learn something Linda had kept hidden that challenged her conscience. And I would see how great a burden it had been, how it defined the person she became, governed the future choices she had made—and revealed the motivation behind wanting "insurance" to protect herself from the Clintons when she taped Monica Lewinsky to avoid being set up in a perjury trap during the Paula Jones case.

———

It was July 20, 1993, less than an hour before the 9:00 a.m. scheduled nomination for Judge Louis Freeh as FBI Director.

The morning sun shone brightly, illuminating the White House. The Rose Garden air was fragrant with the scent of flowers. White folding chairs were clicked out and lined up in perfect rows facing the raised podium bearing the seal of the President of the United States. Stewards completed the finishing touches for the ceremony. The press corps was poised to cover the latest news.

Inside the White House counsel's office, the staffers came in early to race through the last-minute preparations. As Linda recalled it: "Bernie was engaged in his office with Freeh and a handful of his associates from New

Jersey. Janet Reno and Acting FBI Director Floyd Clark were conferring with Al Gore. Betsy [Betsy Pond, Nussbaum's secretary], Deb [Deborah Gorham, Foster's personal secretary], and I were bogged down with last-minute details. Judge Freeh's nomination was so sudden we weren't given much notice to prepare the logistics."

Less than twenty-four hours earlier, President Clinton "hated to be the first president ever to have to fire a director," but he was when he fired FBI Director Williams Sessions on "the recommendation of Janet Reno" after Sessions "refused to resign despite numerous problems within the agency."[161] Not everyone agreed. Director Sessions was at the helm during Travelgate and there were those (predominately on the Right) who saw his firing as a cover-up. The *Wall Street Journal* wrote, "The gang that pulled the great travel office caper is now hell-bent on firing the head of the FBI."[162] Six months later, Sessions released a statement accusing the Clintons of politicizing the FBI, and hampering its ability to investigate Foster's death.[163]

It was just before nine o'clock when an impatient Steve Neuwirth (counsel to the president) called Linda from outside. He asked her to ask Nussbaum what he should do if the press brought up any of the investigations. Linda assumed he meant the travel office, and told him to say what they always did: "We don't comment on ongoing investigations." But Neuwirth apparently was not satisfied, "Look, Linda, I didn't call for your opinion. I want Bernie's."

Linda recalled that Nussbaum was with Freeh and she didn't want to disturb them.

"So then Steve says to me, 'For f–k sake. Linda. Where's Vince?' I told him he was alone in his office, and he insists I interrupt him."

"Did Steve always speak to you like that?" I asked her.

"It wasn't personal," she defended. "I think it had to do with the unbelievable pressures we faced. These Bill and Hillary investigations definitely got the best of us."

Reluctantly, Linda knocked on Foster's door trim. Had it been any other day, Foster would've been in the meeting with Nussbaum and Freeh, but not this day, and that surprised her. That day, Foster was skimming through papers alone when Linda relayed Steve's question. "Sorry to bother you, Vince," she said, "but Steve's on the phone and he wants to know how do we answer press inquiries to the investigations?" Foster looked up at her silently with a blank look. Linda thought he didn't hear her, so she repeated herself, but she received another blank vacant look.

It was unusual to ask him a question twice. "Vince was acting so out of character." Normally, he was the first one with a quick answer, usually answering questions before they were asked. Three times, Linda recalled asking him. "It was like he was a million miles away, so I asked if he was all right."

"You're sure Vince heard you?" I asked her.

"Yes, each time, I spoke louder, until he acknowledged me, but his tone was distant, he said, 'Oh, umm what did you say?' So I repeated Steve's question, and asked for the okay. Finally, Vince answered. 'Yeah, okay. That's fine,' he said."

Judge Freeh's nomination started late. President Clinton's tardiness delayed it until 9:27 a.m. The counsel's office emptied out to the Rose Garden where Linda, Betsy, and Deb watched from the sidelines. Under the podium, senior White House lawyers, except for Foster, gathered with Judge Freeh's wife, their four sons, and the president. Linda's memory was sharp, I crosschecked it against other news accounts when she rattled off the attendees who sat among mainly law enforcement representatives and included Vice President Gore, Attorney General Reno, acting FBI Director Clark and Senator D'Amato.[164] Hillary, who was out of town, out West, was due back in D.C. later that day.

"Vince didn't join his colleagues," Linda remembered. "With a slow gait, he hung back silently, watching nothing in particular." It really bothered her. President Clinton confirmed Linda's recollection of "Foster standing at the back, near one of the grand old magnolia trees planted by Andrew Jackson." Except, President Clinton was not bothered. "Vince had a smile on his face," he wrote, "and I remember thinking he must be relieved that he and the counsel's office were working on things like Supreme Court and FBI appointments, instead of answering endless questions about the travel office."[165]

Judge Freeh, who left his lifetime appointment on the federal bench to head the bureau, made a brief acceptance speech:[166] "At its bedrock, the FBI must stand for absolute integrity, be free of all political influence ... and work solely in the public interest."[167]

Freeh, like Sessions before him, clashed with the Clinton White House in several investigations, including in the "Democratic fund-raising improprieties during Clinton's 1996 re-election."[168] In 2005, Freeh accused President Clinton, "after the 1996 Khobar Towers terrorist attack in Saudi Arabia, where 19 U.S. servicemen died and more than 370 were wounded" of hitting up Crown Prince Abdullah "for a contribution to the Clinton Presidential Library," instead of requesting FBI "access to the suspects the Saudis had arrested."[169]

By 9:40 a.m., the ceremony was over. The stewards began breaking down the chairs while the press corps filed reports. President Clinton and Vice President Gore returned to their offices, and the staffers were back at their desks.

At 10:30 a.m., Foster stepped out of his office, without an explanation. Nor did he offer one when he returned. None of the five Foster investigations could pinpoint where he went. *To get the gun?*

At approximately 11:00 a.m., Gorham (Foster's assistant) hung her purse over her shoulder, and got ready to run out to pick up notary papers for Hillary.

When she reached this point, Linda visibly stiffened as she frequently did when Hillary entered our conversations. She recounted how Gorham was always running out for Hillary. ("Vince wanted her to become a notary to save time," Linda noted.) But this time, Gorham's leaving was different. Support staff covered for one another, practically every day, but Gorham asked her to specifically look out for Foster, which struck Linda as unusual. After verifying that his afternoon calendar was clear, Gorham asked her to remind Foster to eat lunch if she wasn't back in time.

"Why would she ask you to remind Vince to eat?" I asked her.

"Because he was a workaholic, he worked from dusk till dawn," Linda explained, "and often skipped meals."

The White House cafeteria, known as the "mess," could take up to twenty-five minutes to prepare your order. At close to noon, Linda was getting hungry. She popped her head in Foster's office.

"Hungry?" she asked, startling him. Foster looked up from his papers, hesitated, then answered, "Yeah, umm, cheeseburger, fries and a Coke. Thanks."

About ten minutes later Linda and Pond left for the "mess," leaving White House intern Tom Castleton alone with Foster. "I was very clear," Linda insisted. "I told Tom we'd be right back, and not to leave. He was the only one to get the phones."

Shortly thereafter, Linda and Betsy were in the mess line carrying their trays when Linda poured a boatload of M&Ms on Foster's tray hoping to cheer him up, since M&Ms were his favorites. Then out of nowhere and out of breath, Castleton was standing behind her. "Tom, what are you doing here?" Linda asked the intern. A member of support staff was required to be with a lawyer in the counsel's office. Office protocol.

"Vince sent me to get his lunch," Castleton responded.

It didn't make sense to her since Foster, who often forgot to eat, knew how long it took to get lunch. Even more unusual, why would Foster send the remaining staff person out of the office? *Could he have contemplated taking his life then?*

Back at the counsel's office, Foster was waiting at the entrance when they returned upstairs. Linda joked as she handed him his lunch tray, "You must be very hungry to have sent Tom down," and asked again if he was all right.

Vince shuffled his feet, uttering excuses under his breath, claiming he was just hungry. "That's all, thought it was taking a lot of time," he said, brushing off her concerns.

Linda, instinctively, glanced at her watch, as she must've done that day with Vince, reliving it. "I kidded him, 'A lot of time, Vince? You know how long it takes. Are you sure you're all right?'"

But Vince made up another excuse, his head hung heavy, "It's okay, I was just looking for my lunch."

He took his tray into his office, and sat on the loveseat facing his desk, absently flipping through a newspaper, with his back towards the staffers. Linda couldn't help but periodically look over. Vince normally was on the phone, working on a brief, talking into his Dictaphone, loaded with work, and never enough time. "I can't recall him sitting quietly eating lunch before," Linda said. It was not quite 1 p.m. that day.

Minutes later, Linda was barely halfway through her lunch when Vince appeared in the counsel's suite. Smiling broadly, he told her, "Help yourself. There are a lot of M&Ms left." Before she could open her mouth, he hit the door, quickly adding, "I'll be back."

"That was it." Linda said to me, miserably, repeating it, "That was it." That was the last time she saw Vince Foster alive.

Linda was startled by his quick departure because she couldn't imagine where he was going. There were no appointments in his closely kept calendar. Then a funny feeling hit her in the pit of her stomach, but she threw it off. Going into his office to grab some M&Ms, she found he had eaten maybe one.

Later that afternoon, Gorham returned from her errands, stymied and kept saying, "There's nothing on the book. Where did Vince go?"

"All I could say was he wouldn't say," Linda said, shrugging her shoulders. "He looked like he had an appointment. Maybe he's meeting someone in the building."

More than two hours passed. Now it was after 3 p.m., and the counsel's office hummed with its usual heavy workload. Nussbaum and the other lawyers had long since returned from lunch, but there was still no word from Foster when Linda remembered Nussbaum paging him. "They were rarely out of contact and it wasn't like Vince not to check in. Bernie was concerned," Linda said.

The day after Foster's body was found in Fort Marcy Park, White House Chief of Communications Director Mark Gearan was asked at a press briefing, "Was it unusual for [Foster] to be out of the office all afternoon? Did he say anything to anyone before he left the White House?"

"He did not," Gearan answered. "He said he would be back."[170] Two other reporters pressed for more. Each time Gearan reiterated, "At different points ... Bernie said, 'Is he back yet?' But it was not atypical. It was not viewed as any way unusual. ... They weren't sure of his exact schedule."[171]

But that wasn't true.

"Think about it—what job doesn't require their staff checking in?" Linda countered, "This is the White House. Staff, especially senior staff, always remain in touch. They have to. You never know when something of world consequence may occur." Growing visibly annoyed, she reinforced her argument, "Deb always knew Vince's schedule, just like I knew Bernie's. Even, support staff—all of us had to coordinate our schedules so someone was in the office."

"So when the reporter asked if someone paged Vince, and Mark answered 'no,' is that true?" I asked Linda.

"No. Bernie paged Vince," she said.

Worried, from what Linda observed, Nussbaum was concerned for a while. They weren't merely colleagues but friends, "almost brothers," and workaholics, who relied heavily on one another and were rarely out of touch. "I can't remember how many times Bernie and Deb asked about Vince. It's outrageous and insulting that the White House would suggest otherwise." Linda exclaimed, "We racked our brains trying to figure out where Vince went, and tried to find him. I was running out of logical excuses, worried myself. We all were."

"Was Mark in the counsel's office that day?" I asked.

"Not that I know of," Linda replied.

"So, his press briefing is not a firsthand account. Is it fair to say Mark may not have known?" I asked.

"Possible," she conceded. "He was following orders. No one who speaks on behalf of the White House goes before the press until they're briefed on what to say. He told the press what the Clintons wanted the public to hear."

The issue as to whether or not Nussbaum paged Foster may seem small, even irrelevant, but it was not irrelevant to the White House, which denied it had happened.

According to a U.S. Park Police evidence control receipt, Foster's pager, discovered in the off position, was attached to the belt he was wearing when his body was found.[172] Other personal property, such as his wallet, rings, and watch, were released to the White House on the evening of July 21 to be returned his family.[173] Typically, the next of kin is given the deceased's personal belongings *after* a thorough investigation is conducted to rule out any question of foul play. The handling of Foster's belongings—forensically un-tested, unique—fed the conspiracy beast. It could never be proven whether it was Foster or somebody else who turned off his pager. Fingerprints were not lifted off any of his personal belongings either.

Four years after Foster's death, Starr found, "White House records of pager messages do not indicate messages sent to or from Mr. Foster,"[174] a finding which would negate Linda's memory, except later in Starr's report we learned that, "complete [White House] records ... are not available."[175] *Why would the White House withhold records?*

Starr was not alone in his frustrated attempt to obtain documentation from the Clinton White House. The Senate Whitewater Committee ran into the same obstacle during their investigation.

Two-and-a-half years after Foster's death, on January 22, 1996, the committee found "because the testimony of witnesses ... was often contradictory, the committee has placed particular emphasis on available documentary evidence. Unfortunately, the committee has been hindered by parties unduly delaying the production of, or withholding outright, documents critical to [the Foster] investigation."[176]

History repeats itself. In 2011, the Obama administration snubbed House Rep. Darrell Issa's House Oversight and Government Reform Committee's request for documents from Obama's Department of Homeland Security (DHS)."Issa charges that top DHS officials actually instructed career employees not to search for the documents he is requesting."[177]

Was Linda telling the truth? Did Bernie page Vince? It's a possibility and can't be ruled out. What was the big deal about admitting to paging a colleague when no one knew where he was? Moreover, isn't withholding documents (that also occurred during Travelgate) obstruction of justice?

For Linda, Deb, and Betsy it had been a long day. And, unbeknownst to them, July 20, 1993, was far from over. It was just beginning. Late afternoon, the ladies left the president's lawyers and headed for home. By then, Lisa, Foster's wife, had called looking for her husband, but there still was no word from him.

Linda left Bernie, with no out-of-office meetings scheduled on his calendar that night. At 5:59 p.m., a park service employee contacted 911 and reported that a possible dead body had been found in Fort Marcy Park.[178] Mid-flight to D.C. from the West Coast, Hillary made an unscheduled stop in Arkansas "between 8-9 p.m.," as she wrote in her book, "to drop off her mother and visit some friends."[179]

Chapter 9: The Foster Investigations

"You shall not circulate a false report. Do not put
your hand with the wicked to be an unrighteous witness."

—Exodus 23:1 (NKJV)

Imagine being the president of the United States, or the First Lady, and discovering that your friend, your best friend, was found dead in a park. More than a valued colleague, he had grieved with you when your father had died.[180] He had celebrated your White House victory. He'd been your rock of Gibraltar and uprooted his life and his family to serve in your administration.[181] His wife taught your daughter how to swim. His children were your child's friends.[182]

Let's assume that you have the good fortune to sit in America's highest office with advantages the average person doesn't enjoy—unlimited access to top investigative offices, the CIA and FBI, the world's top experts one phone call away. With the stroke of a pen you had issued executive orders that overturned statutes. But instead of using this power, these resources, to find out everything about your friend's death, you leave it to the U.S. Park Police to investigate before anyone could know with reasonable confidence that no foul play was involved.

Oddly, during five investigations spanning four years, the Clinton White House never turned over documents that investigators sought to help them do their job. Instead, if the official findings were challenged, and hearings were held like the "Republican senators and their staffs conducted," on Foster's death, as Hillary wrote in her book, *Living History,* they "inflicted great emotional and monetary damage on innocent people."[183]

Individuals with fewer resources have done more to find out everything there was to know about the sudden and shocking death of a friend or loved one, than did the Clintons for their "dear" friend. Some of their stories appear on shows like NBC's *Dateline,* ABC's *20/20* and *Primetime Live,* CBS's *48 Hour Mystery;* and on *Fox News, CNN,* and *MSNBC.*

By contrast, consider the history of the Foster investigations.

The day after Foster died, Press Secretary Dee Dee Myers told the press about the U.S. Park Police investigation—the first investigation. "It is a fairly limited investigation," she said, "the Park Service was just looking into—again to establish—to confirm what they believe was a suicide."[184] From the get-go, homicide, foul play, the possibility of blackmail, a potential risk to national security, were never investigated. As a government official, principally one who worked with the First Family, it's reasonable to assume and expect that a closer look was warranted.

Because Foster was found dead in a National Park, the case belonged to the Park Police, part of the Department of the Interior. The FBI, which normally would have and could have investigated such a death, was sidelined. Two days after Foster's death, on July 22, 1993, Linda's boss, Nussbaum, on behalf of the counsel's office, requested that the Justice Department coordinate Foster's investigation with the Park Police.[185] It sounded good.

One week later, "the Justice Department backed off its pledge to conduct a full investigation" and said "it was merely participating in a low-level inquiry" run by the Park Police.[186] The Park Police concluded Foster committed suicide in Fort Marcy Park.

The second investigation began nearly six months after Foster's death, on January 20, 1994. Under pressure from Congress, Attorney General Reno appointed Independent Counsel Robert Fiske Jr. to launch an investigation in conjunction with Whitewater. Fiske released his report on June 30, 1994, agreeing with the Park Police's assessment. On February 24, 1994, seven months after Foster's death, Republican Congressman William F. Clinger Jr. initiated his inquiry. It was the third Foster investigation. Clinger released his report on August 12, 1994, endorsing the Park Police findings based on "all the available facts."[187]

Next it was the Senate Banking Committee's turn: the fourth Foster investigation. The bipartisan committee, also known as the Senate Whitewater Committee, held hearings on July 29, 1994.

Fourteen months after Foster's death, on August 5, 1994, the fifth and final investigation began when newly appointed Kenneth Starr's Independent Counsel launched an inquiry.

Two years since Foster's death, in the summer of 1995, the Senate Banking Committee "overwhelmingly" concurred with Fiske's second conclusion, which was affirmed by the Park Police's first investigation. On October 10, 1997, four years after Foster died, Starr agreed with Fiske's conclusion, which was affirmed by the Park Police's investigation. Indeed, Foster committed suicide in Fort Marcy Park. He was depressed. Case closed, so it seemed.

Except the problems with the Park Police's initial investigation (the foundation for the next four investigations) began instantly; and immediately raised unanswered questions.

For openers, evidence gathering where Foster's body was found was at best poorly handled, as Starr wrote, "The collection and preservation of physical evidence is [sic] the most important building blocks available to the crime scene investigator."[188] In Foster's case, the 35mm photographs that Park Police took off his body "were underexposed and of little value."[189] Because Foster's "clothing was packaged together before trace evidence was collected, specific trace evidence cannot be conclusively linked to particular items of clothing [that Foster] was wearing at the time of his death."[190] The medical examiner's laboratory "intended to take x-rays," of Foster's body but the lab's new x-ray machine was "not functioning properly."[191] No alternative arrangements were made. Foster was buried three days after he died.

"A perfect reconstruction ... was not possible," wrote Dr. Henry Lee, famed Director of the Connecticut State Police Forensic Science Laboratory, when he was commissioned by Starr to help in his investigation. Lee, known for the O.J. Simpson case, wrote: "The reasons include the lack of complete documentation of the original shooting scene; the lack of subsequent records and photographs of each item of physical evidence prior to examinations; the lack of documentation of the amount of blood, tissue, and bone fragments in the areas at the scene under and around Foster's head; the lack of close-up photographs of any definite patterns and quantity of the blood stains on Foster's clothing and body at the scene; and the unknown location of the fatal bullet, which makes complete reconstruction of the bullet trajectory difficult."[192]

Based on the Park Police's failure at evidence gathering, common sense would say there was only one reasonable conclusion that all the Foster inquiries should have reached: it was not possible to decisively conclude what had happened to Vince Foster.

Both Starr and Fiske attempted to recover evidence and complete what the original investigation had missed or failed to do. Starr sent investigators to the neighborhood around Fort Marcy Park because there was "no record of any effort to canvass the neighborhood near the time of death to determine whether anyone had seen or heard relevant information."[193] Another failed attempt brought Fiske and Starr's investigators back to the park to locate physical evidence, specifically the fatal bullet and bone fragments from Foster's skull. Investigators recovered bullets and other metal objects, but none of the bullets was the one that killed Foster. During Fiske's inquiry, agents screened and sifted through approximately 18 inches down into the soil, and found "no bone fragments" that belonged to Foster.[194]

Taking into account the indisputable failures of the Park Police's unreliable investigation, who had confidently accepted the official Foster findings? Hillary and Bill Clinton. Did Linda trust those findings?

"No, of course not. How can anyone trust it? That's why it's so chilling," she answered. "The official version is what the Clintons wanted everyone to believe." [195]

Bill Clinton wrote in *My Life* that he "was glad Fiske was looking at [Foster's death]. The scandal machine was trying to get blood out of a turnip and maybe this would shut them up and give Vince's family some relief." [196]

When Foster's death fell under Starr's purview, President Clinton grew impatient: "Starr showed his 'independence' when unbelievably he said he was going to reinvestigate Vince Foster's death."[197] In 957 pages of President Clinton's memoir, there are no references of concern or outrage over the outrageously flawed evidence gathering done by the Park Police.

For Hillary, like her husband, the official Foster findings are untouchable. When it came to Starr, Hillary described him as the "part-timer; [with] zero criminal law experience, who was learning on the job."[198] Yet

Hillary was satisfied when, "Starr had finally conceded that Vince Foster really had committed suicide."[199] Why would Hillary trust the 'part-timer with zero criminal law experience' now?

It should have taken one competent investigation to resolve the death of a senior White House official and end reasonable speculation. Instead Bill and Hillary deemed the "official findings" as truth based on the slap-dash investigative work of the Park Police.

But placing blame on the Park Police would be unfair. Like their successors during Travelgate, they confronted obstruction-like tactics from the Clinton White House. According to Thomas Collier, the chief of staff of the Secretary of the Interior, "The Park Police" were "very, very, upset about the investigation ... [and] that they really couldn't get the cooperation [from the White House] that they wanted to their superiors."[200]

The day after Foster's death, on July 21, 1993, at 12:50 p.m., before a reasonable investigation was conducted, President Clinton at a press briefing said, "In times of difficulty [Foster] was normally the Rock of Gibraltar while other people were having trouble. No one could ever remember the reverse being the case. ... I don't know if we'll ever know [what happened to Foster]... and because no one can know why things like this happen [suicide]... we'll just have to live with something else we can't understand."[201]

Later that day, at 3:30 p.m. Chief of Staff McLarty parroted President Clinton, "For try as we might all of our reason, all of our rationality, all of our logic can never answer the questions raised by such a death." [202]

The next day, Press Secretary Myers added her voice to the echo chamber, "I think it's been our position that it's impossible to know. ... It is a mystery, and I think the president made that very clear yesterday. It is a mystery." [203]

Then Stephanopoulos, replicating the president, told the *Post*, "Since you can't ever know, it's impossible to speculate on it. In the end, it is a mystery."[204]

The Park Police officially declared Foster's death a suicide, over two weeks later, on August 10, 1993.[205]

"It was too soon for the White House to know what happened," Linda maintained. "They could've told us he was found dead in the park. 'Looks like a suicide ... we're investigating.' But no, they wanted me, all the staffers, the American people to believe their version, now."

Linda had a point. Typically when a scandal broke, Bill and Hillary cautioned the public to wait until the facts came out before drawing any conclusions. Their reaction to Foster's death was the opposite.

During the Lewinsky-Clinton scandal, for example, Hillary said, "The best thing to do in these cases is just to be patient, take a deep breath, and the truth will come out."[206] Bill wanted evidence during Filegate (another Clinton investigation where hundreds of FBI files in a "bureaucratic snafu" ended up in the Clinton White House).[207] "Until I have evidence to the contrary—and I mean evidence," the president said, "we need evidence before we draw any conclusions."[208]

After the media cried foul, Linda recalled how the original cohesive strategy crafted in the counsel's office was revised from, "Found dead in Fort Marcy Park, suicide, we didn't see it coming," to "Found dead in Fort Marcy Park, suicide, Vince was depressed."[209]

Then the classic defense, (part of the three talking points), the Clintons used to combat all the investigations was deployed: "Nothing here, it's our political enemies bent on destroying us, stupid."

As Linda recalled, it doubled as the language the presidential counsel lawyers used to prep the staffers on how to testify. Like Travelgate, staffers were ordered not to speculate or offer information on Foster. It went like this: "The investigators are on a political witch hunt. So make it short and sweet and get out. They're trying to take down the president." Except, Foster was found dead less than twenty-four hours earlier. Perhaps the investigators wanted to do their jobs and investigate Foster's death—not play politics with the Clintons.

Hillary and Obama's guru Saul Alinsky instructed that a successful organizer must have an organized personality: "so he can be comfortable in a disorganized situation, rational in a sea of irrationalities. It is vital that he be able to accept and work with irrationalities for the purpose of change."[210]

When the staffers were questioned by Park Police investigators, Linda knew they weren't going to get much. "I wanted to tell them everything, but nobody could," she said because the staffers were accompanied by an associate White House counsel. *Why won't the Clintons let us speculate or offer information that might be helpful to the investigation? Don't they want to know what happened to Vince?* She wondered. With a sick sense of déjà-vu, an aura of "cover-up" surrounded her, yet she followed the Clinton White House orders (the cohesive strategy) on how to speak to investigators. Uncomfortable and intimidated, her justification loop played like this: serving at the White House was an honor and privilege. She wanted to stay, hoped to do good ... her job, her pension, and her kids ...

"It felt wrong, really wrong. Nobody likes to have Hillary's henchmen breathing down their neck. None of us did," Linda bristled as she justified herself. "The Park Police found my White House 'escort' as disconcerting as I did," she said. Her White House escort assured their quizzical faces, "We're just here to make sure everything is recorded accurately."

Fearing retaliation, Linda sat down and played by the Clintons' rules to keep her job at the expense of helping investigators learn what happened to Foster. She hated it, and she ate nonstop afterwards, but she did it. She said she had no choice. Now on the record, she, like other staffers were bound in unholy alliance to the Clintons that appears throughout all the Foster inquiries. As the Senate Whitewater Committee investigation confirms, the investigators "faced numerous instances where witnesses provided inconsistent or contradictory testimony, and even more often ... [said] 'I don't recall' or 'I have no specific recollection or knowledge' relating to crucial facts."[211]

Just like occurred during the Park Police's investigation where Foster's body was found, the problems for investigators with Hillary's counsel's office surfaced immediately and never stopped. The lack of cooperation with investigators was so outrageously suspicious that even Clinton-appointed Deputy Attorney General Phillip Heymann confronted Linda's boss, Bernie Nussbaum, demanding to know if he were "hiding something."[212]

Saul Alinsky commanded, "Ethical standards must be elastic to stretch with the time." According to his eighth rule of means and ends ethics: "In short, ethics are determined by whether one is losing or winning."[213]

The passage of time in any investigation is never kind. Leads run cold. Memories fade. Forensic evidence vanishes. One cannot undo the bungled evidence-collection that initially occurred during the Foster investigation. Neither Starr nor Fiske, despite their attempts, could turn back time and re-collect precious evidence where Foster's body was found or where he was last seen alive. Forced to draw a conclusion using the incomplete, contaminated evidence and conflicting stonewalling testimony from the White House they had, the OIC investigators had no alternative but to draw the most logical explanation—but logical does not always mean an accurate conclusion.

Contrary to what the Clintons, the mainstream press and their defenders say, all this raises serious questions about what really happened to Vince Foster. It lays credence to the so-called conspiracy theories, and gives in to tides of lawlessness.

Five years later during the Lewinsky-Clinton investigation, Linda testified: "I had reason to believe that the Vince Foster tragedy was not depicted accurately under oath by members of the administration ... and these are, remember, instances of national significance that included testimony by Mrs. Clinton, also in Travelgate. It became very important for them for their version of events to be the accepted version of events, I knew based on my personal knowledge, personal observations that they were lying under oath. So it became very fearful for me that I had information even back then that was very dangerous." [214] She had reason to believe because she was a part of it to keep her job. "I told you we were told what to say," she snapped back at me after a slip. It had tormented her ever since.

Here again, contrary to conventional wisdom that Linda was a whistleblower, she had been loyal to the Clintons to protect her job. Towing the Clinton line during the Foster investigations played a major role in the motivation behind why she wanted "insurance" to protect herself from the Clintons when she taped Monica Lewinsky—she didn't want to cover for the Clintons anymore. She hadn't had insurance to back up the truth during the earlier investigations when she'd served in the Clinton White House.

As Foster eloquently stated before his untimely death, "Before we came here we thought of ourselves as good people." [215]

The First Amendment to the United States Constitution states: "Congress shall make no law ... abridging the freedom of speech, or of the press ...." In the Clintons' America, an unwritten law was manifesting. [216] Asking obvious questions about the Foster death investigation became taboo. Honest reporting was attacked. [217] If anyone strayed from the Clinton White House version of events, they may expect to be ridiculed, vilified, and dismissed as a right-wing hack or scolded by Hillary for inflicting "great emotional and monetary damage on innocent people," effectively silencing legitimate questions (freedom of speech) about the death of a senior official who served in the People's house. [218] Americans no longer had a right to know what was happening in their White House.

Diminishing critical thinking and common sense, the Clinton White House repeatedly told the public what to think about Foster's death until it stuck and became the "truth." As the investigations dragged on, people tuned out. For the most part, the elite media bought it; or they played along perhaps to get access to America's First Family. Notice how the press didn't bring up the obvious glaring problems with the Foster case or Travelgate with Hillary when she ran for president in 2008.

The day after Foster's death marked the beginning of the end. Life at the Clinton White House changed forever. For several staffers, including Linda and her boss, Nussbaum, their days serving in the Clinton White House were coming to a close.

Chapter 10: Nothing Here, Move Along ...

"But for those who are self-seeking and self-willed and disobedient to the Truth but responsive to wickedness, there will be indignation and wrath."

—Romans 2:8 (AMP)

This is where the plot thickens and more facts collide with the Clintons' historical revisionism. It was the fall of 1993 when Hillary's White House counsel's office was given a mendacious heads-up to the latest so-called political enemy attack against the Clintons. This one was called "RTC" and crashed into Whitewater where it stayed muddled in controversy marked by indictments throughout the Clintons' two terms in office.

Resolution Trust Corporation (RTC) was a federal agency responsible for cleaning up the savings and loan default of Madison Guaranty, which was controlled by the Clintons' Whitewater partners, James and Susan McDougal. When RTC requested the Justice Department investigate Madison Guaranty's financial stability, lending practices, and potential illegal transactions (including campaign donations to then Governor Clinton's campaign), huge problems erupted. First, the press discovered there was a conflict of interest. RTC reported to an old Clinton friend, Deputy Treasury Secretary Roger Altman.[219] Next, Clinton aides, including Linda's boss, were tipped off by Treasury Department officials "about the progress of the RTC investigation."[220]

History repeats itself. Like Madison Guaranty was bailed out costing U.S. taxpayers $73 million, Fannie Mae and Freddie Mac (backed by the federal government) during the housing crisis were bailed out by taxpayers to the "tune of $160 billion." [221]

At that time, with Vince Foster's recent death, a renewed and vigorous media interest in Whitewater was hitting critical mass. The *New York Times* and the *Washington Post* now wanted to review all Whitewater documents. After Foster's death, Hillary eventually testified it was Foster who retained Madison Guaranty as a Rose Law Firm client.[222] Livid, Linda scowled when we discussed it, "Sure, blame the dead guy."

Meanwhile, inside the counsel's office, the staffers—who were still reeling from Foster's death while combating ghoulish cover-up speculation—met twice daily to tackle the press. RTC eclipsed their grief and became part of their jobs. It was because, as usual, Hillary insisted they withhold all Whitewater documents from the press, Linda recalled.

Even Hillary acknowledged the stress in her memoir, and wrote: "Harold Ickes, an old friend and adviser from the 1992 campaign, had joined the administration as Deputy Chief of Staff ... to coordinate the upcoming health care reform. Within days, he was diverted to organize a 'Whitewater Response Team' (nicknamed the Masters of Disasters) composed of several senior advisors and members of the communications staff and counsel's office ... Harold did his best to keep the Whitewater debate under control but the turmoil continued in the West Wing."[223] Ickes, Hillary's "hammer," and a famed political-street fighter, would go on to spearhead her 2008 failed presidential bid.[224]

Saul Alinsky's tenth rule: The major premise for tactics is the development of operations that will maintain a constant pressure upon the opposition.[225] In 2011, the Obama administration "created and staffed a new position" to coordinate rapid response to unfavorable press and also launched a website, "Attackwatch.com."[226]

As fall turned to winter in December 1993, the Clinton White House continued stonewalling the press. With the public growing increasingly suspicious of the Clintons' secrecy, the White House agreed "to turn over Whitewater documents to the Justice Department" (where political appointees serve at the pleasure of the president) instead of giving them to the press for review. This action was at best a misleading PR stunt to silence public doubts because the Justice Department "had been preparing to subpoena them."[227]

But it was too little, too late. Calls for reinstating the Independent Counsel Statute to investigate Whitewater poured in. If the Clintons were innocent and Whitewater wasn't nefarious, why was the White House behaving as if it were? The calls grew louder after the Clinton White House concocted another stall tactic. They needed time to *first* catalogue the Whitewater papers *before* handing them over to Justice.

Perplexed, Linda went to her boss. "Why don't they appoint a special prosecutor? It looks like they're hiding something."

Nussbaum admonished her: "Hillary won't let us. We can't limit their scope of investigation."

By then, Linda knew "because Hillary doesn't want it" ended all discussions. She was not unique in that knowledge. Reportedly, "Hillary's word was law." As one top administration official described it: "If Mama's not happy, nobody is happy." [228]

Sure, Linda could understand that Hillary didn't want their private lives scrutinized, but it comes with holding office. If you've nothing to hide, who cares? Why duck full disclosure and subject the taxpayer-salaried staffers to act as your personal buffers and spears in the endless task of protecting your financial shenanigans?

Stephanopoulos also smacked into that barricade after he argued for full disclosure. "Bernie Nussbaum, David Kendall (Clinton's private attorney), and Hillary had persuaded the president to stonewall ... determined to follow a close-hold strategy more appropriate for corporate litigation than presidential politics."[229]

In an interview, Press Secretary Myers also backed up Linda's recollection when she recalled how Stephanopoulos made the mistake of challenging Hillary. She said this: "And George began to make the argument that we'd all been making and nobody backed him up ... Everyone just sat there and let George take the beating ... And Mrs. Clinton got really angry. She attacked George, which everyone knew was coming, which is why I guess nobody was willing to ride in there to the rescue ... But there's no talking her out of it. ... And anybody that stood up and tried to say this was a bad idea was, you know, [was] smashed down and belittled, very personally ...."[230]

"We all knew if we challenged the Clintons there would be hell to pay," Linda confirmed. "You're challenging the leader of the free world and his wife, the co-president."

To understand the Clintons' marriage, consider the supporting roles the Clintons play to protect one another—depending on who is the scandal star of the day. Look at Hillary's Whitewater stonewall defended by her husband, and Bill's Monica Lewinsky stonewall, defended by his wife. Where Bill, in mortal combat, like Hillary during Whitewater, refused to cooperate with investigators or the media until forensics (Bill's semen on Monica's dress) forced him to.

It was January 1994 when Linda was asked to stay late because another blistering Whitewater story was about to hit the press. Linda and the counsel office lawyers, already frayed from months of working Clinton damage control, braced themselves again. Skeletons kept escaping from the Clintons' closet and each time the staffers shoved one back in, two more appeared. With or without Hillary's blessing, an independent counsel would be appointed.

"We can't contain this any longer," Nussbaum told the room that included top guns like David Kendall, and senior presidential aide Bruce Lindsey, Linda remembered. Lindsey presently serves as Chief Executive Officer of the William J. Clinton Foundation.[231]

But how the news played to Americans was something the White House *could* control. Requesting a special counsel, *as if* it were the White House's idea, a PR maneuver, would create the *appearance* of cooperation to the public.

That night, Linda supported the lawyers as they painstakingly wrote a letter to Attorney General Janet Reno. The burden of that historic decision weighed heavily upon them in part because they'd have to deal with the wreckage and fallout for Hillary—but there was no turning back now.

The letter said: "The president has directed me to request you to appoint as special counsel a respected, impartial and qualified attorney, who is not a member of the Department of Justice or an employee of the federal government to conduct an appropriate independent investigation of the Whitewater matter and report to the American people."[232]

With precision everything was planned. Afterward, Linda hurried to the Justice Department to hand deliver the letter. The second Attorney

General Reno had it, as instructed, Linda called the White House to notify them. Then Stephanopoulos broke the story. It made the morning news.

On January 20, 1994, the media reported, "Attorney General Janet Reno names New York lawyer and former U.S. attorney Robert B. Fiske Jr. as special counsel to investigate the Clintons' involvement in Whitewater. Fiske ... will also explore a potential link between Foster's suicide ...." [233]

Meanwhile, more suspicious news surfaced. In March 1994, the media had been in an uproar when it came to light that Hillary's Rose Law firm in Arkansas had shredded documents—one box had had Vince Foster's initials on it. Then, two years later, billing records under Congressional subpoena surfaced at the residence that showed "that Mrs. Clinton billed Madison Guaranty Savings and Loan, a client of the Rose firm, for about 60 hours of work over 15 months," something she had long denied. [234]

As usual, the Clintons brushed everything off. As Bill wrote in his memoir; "... the media was wringing its hands about some documents ... The firm explained that the shredding involved material unrelated to Whitewater and was a normal procedure." [235]

But the brush-offs and duplicity persisted throughout the Clinton administration and beyond. Both Bill and Hillary rewrote history in their memoirs. Bill claimed, "We didn't resist subpoenas and we turned all our records over to the Justice Department and then to Fiske."[236]

Hillary backed up her husband while typically blaming political adversaries, "Bill and I voluntarily cooperated with investigators. Every time they leaked or leveled a new charge, we bent over backwards to make sure we hadn't missed or overlooked anything ... Whitewater signaled a new tactic in political warfare; investigation as a weapon for political destruction."[237]

But behind the bluster of the Clintons' rewrites, a vastly different story was unfolding, according to Linda. There was much more hand-wringing going on in the counsel's office that the press and the public didn't know about.

Following orders that she did not feel were routine, Linda told me that documents weren't only being shredded in Arkansas but in the White House—and names were being purged from computer phone records. She proceeded to describe the tricky business of trying to tell the truth in a careful way; and attempting to satisfy subpoena requests for documents.

"Hillary treated every leak and leveled new charge as a fatal attack," Linda grumbled. "All the staffers had no choice but to follow Hillary's orders." Her gut told her it was wrong. She didn't want to do it but she did. "If you questioned Hillary you were attacked like a political opponent," Linda said, rationalizing, justifying her actions.

Here again, Linda's conscience took flight as Whitewater and RTC flung her back onto that teetering tight-rope (which first appeared during Travelgate) of trying to keep her job without sacrificing all her ethics and values. But that was impossible; her moral decay continued.

Was Linda lying about the Clinton White House withholding and destroying Whitewater evidence or did the Clintons lie to the public?

Look at what OIC Special Prosecutor Robert Ray (who succeeded Starr and Fiske) found in his Final Whitewater Report in 2001, "the White House has failed to produce all documents to which this Office is entitled." [238] Because the Clintons withheld evidence, evidence destruction cannot be ruled out. Moreover, the OIC concluded that the Clintons made statements to the investigators that were "factually inaccurate," which may also explain why there was insufficient evidence to bring charges against them. [239]

Now we see another tactic the Clintons used to stay in power and dodge indictments: withholding evidence to thwart investigations. Even a non-lawyer would be inclined to think "obstruction of justice."

During the Whitewater investigations, the Clinton White House turned the public view away from the truth. The question which must be asked is this: would a member of the general public, the average citizen, have walked away free after withholding evidence or making false statements, or would they have been held in contempt or possibly jailed for obstructing justice? In the Clintons' America, it appears that a special class, with a "special rights justice system" was created for the ruling class. Demanding team-player blind loyalty from those who served under the Clintons made it possible.

Instead of swift justice and a legal system that immediately held officials and White House staffers accountable whenever they stonewalled investigators, ignored subpoenas, or retaliated against a truth-teller, an emboldened Clinton administration kept stalling and playing by its own rules until the country lost interest and tuned out. Ask yourself this: Are Bill, Hillary, and government employees above the law? Is anyone? Linda, against her better judgment once again, remained a Clinton team player.

It is necessary to question the point at which an individual must draw the line, resign and—blow the whistle. When does the moral imperative outweigh rationalization? If it never does and you don't stand tall against corruption, then is it fair to say you become just as corrupt? The honor of serving at the White House was no longer a privilege. It was a nightmare, chiseling away at Linda's conscious, destroying who she once was. She wanted redemption now and to make things right by finally telling the whole truth.

As Linda bluntly admitted, "… with all the different investigations I felt like I had been a team player. It bothered my sense of values—it did—it bothered me, but I was selfish. I wanted my job. I wanted my livelihood. So for security I shut up."[240]

History repeats itself. Except unlike Linda, in 2010, J. Christian Adams, a Department of Justice voting rights lawyer, resigned in protest after President Obama's Justice Department's stonewalling and refusal to prosecute a case "involving voter intimidation by the New Black Panther Party" that was caught on tape.[241]

Linda's admitted sell-out to protect the Clintons, while straying from her Christian faith, and from what she knew was right and honest, granted her another temporary employment reprieve. But that's all it would be—a temporary reprieve, because unbeknownst to her, Bill and Hillary's Svengali roles were about to switch in another upcoming Clinton scandal, one that would sweep Linda up in it, when Paula Jones accused President Clinton of sexual harassment.

Chapter 11: Smoke and Mirrors

"At that time if anyone says to you, 'Look, here is the Messiah!' or, 'There he is!' do not believe it. For false messiahs and false prophets will appear and perform great signs and wonders to deceive, if possible, even the elect."

—Matthew 24:23-24 (NIV)

It was the spring of 1994 when the horrific genocide in Rwanda, Africa, broke out. The Central African ethnic group the Hutus, attempted to exterminate the Tutsis. The slaughter of 800,000 people started in April and lasted 100 days until June.[242] In 1998 that tragedy brought Bill and Hillary to Rwanda where Bill said, "All over the world there were people like me ... who did not fully appreciate ... [that] you were being engulfed in this unimaginable terror."[243]

For Linda, something very disturbing was happening in the Clinton White House that spring. Fighting the Clinton's so-called political enemies had left Hillary's Rose Law Firm colleagues and friends within the administration in calamity. The cost and toll were undeniable. Foster was dead. Hubbell, the third-highest official in the Justice Department, was prison-bound. Linda's boss, the loyal Nussbaum, resigned that March, disgraced and humiliated.[244]

"Bernie resigned at a time when there were questions about the investigation of Vince Foster's suicide," said Special Counsel Jane Sherburne, who was brought in after he left. "There was a perception that [Foster and

Whitewater] issues had been mishandled ... that they needed someone to come in who would restore some confidence, that there was a real grown-up in there."[245]

"Bernie was following Hillary's orders," Linda gloomily said, defending her boss. "He was forced to resign. He resisted resigning initially, although he knew it was inevitable."

Nussbaum paid for the honor and privilege of serving in the Clinton White House by apparently taking on the role of the fall guy, yet another stay-in-power tactic. Meanwhile Foster's assistant, Deb Gorham, had left. Gone too was Betsy Pond. Linda comforted herself with food.

History repeats itself. In 2011, during the gun-running operation called "Fast and Furious," acting ATF Director Kenneth Melson was pressured to take the fall and resign. He has since been reassigned to a lesser post in the Justice Department.[246] Obama's Attorney General Eric Holder, who served as deputy attorney general during the Clinton administration, and was involved in President Clinton's last minute dubious pardons, isn't saying who authorized the program. Hillary's State Department is also stonewalling investigators.[247]

But Linda was also angry.[248] She resented the "protect-the-Clintons-at-anyone's-expense" that her job had become. She appeared to be living in the world of *the ends justifies the means*, another Saul Alinsky Machiavellian lesson. "The means-and-end-moralists or non-doers always wind up on their ends without any means," he chided.[249] Nevertheless, Linda tiptoed around, clutching her job, while new lawyers moved into the counsel's office. They "all became Hillary's personal lawyers," she said.

Incredibly, a deceptive sense of safety continued to fool Linda into believing that as a Clinton team player she'd be secure; her job would be secure even though that false belief was challenged by feelings of endangerment. By then she knew she (or anybody) could be disposed of as collateral damage to keep the Clintons in power.

Meanwhile, the Clintons vowed to fight for Americans and stand up to their political opponents. But that would only be possible if their staffers could keep them out of jail and themselves handcuff free.

It was also that April in 1994 when Hillary's approval ratings plunged after a steady diet of bad press, zeroing in on her Whitewater dealings, and her fishy role as the unelected co-president. Even worse for the counsel staffers, that March had brought forth more mindboggling news. Hillary had magically parlayed a $1,000 commodities futures investment into a $99,540 windfall which she chalked up to luck.[250]

While Rwanda burned, inside the White House it was damage control time again. The counsel office lawyers convened. Their verdict was unanimous: Hillary must boost those polling numbers.

When Linda arrived at work she was told to cancel whatever was on the schedule because there was an emergency. *An emergency? World crisis? Upheaval with Congress over legislation?* No, the emergency was Hillary. The counsel's office was going to hold a press conference, she was notified.

Should she call the press office, she offered, since the press office handles press conferences? No, this was the Clinton White House—this emergency was a counsel's office production. Linda Bloodworth-Thomason and her husband, Harry, creators of *Designing Women*, and of Travelgate fame, were brought in to produce it. Linda began her latest counsel's office's mission resigned to its public relations damage-control role.

President Clinton's remarkable craft is public speaking. In any camera, he could speak soft, yet firm. His lower lip could protrude or hinge upwards showing determination. His purposeful pauses; a gentle smile or a clenched jaw; contrition or empathy tears were always on cue—unlike Hillary.

Linda recounted how for days the Hollywood power couple held rehearsals with Hillary in the counsel's office while the press office was sidelined to the logistics and lights-camera technical side. The support staff was told to hold the lawyers' calls.

Because Hillary's natural inclination was to be combative, everyone worked late. Locations, props, and outfits were kicked around and evaluated. The overriding question: "What would be the most believable to the American people?"

"She's the First Lady," said one of the lawyers, "We don't want her standing at the podium in the press room. It'll look too much like the co-president thing. We need to soften her, make her a real wife, maybe the residence?"

"Not the West Wing and God forbid, not her office," interjected another White House attorney, who argued among the other lawyers until the winning location was decided upon for where to hold Hillary's press conference; under a portrait of Abe Lincoln next to a roaring fire.

Cast as the First Lady, as opposed to the co-president involved in questionable financial dealings, Linda watched the Thomasons with Hillary's inner circle pepper her with questions, drilling her through an acting crash course that would've brought the legendary acting coach Stella Adler to tears.

As Hillary awkwardly settled into a chair, some of her coaching tips included, "Cross your legs, remember, ladies fold their hands in their laps. No, no, no, head back. No, lean forward, relax, relax ... soften, soften, soften." Leaving nothing to chance, Linda detailed how Hillary was prepped on the tone she should adopt; when and how to smile, show her teeth; not show her teeth and how to look hurt on cue. "I want your hair off your face, open, open, you're not trying to hide anything and that's the message. This Whitewater is 'much ado about nothing,'" Linda mimicked to me.

Hillary resented it, hated it, but she'd do what she had to do to get it right.

After each rehearsal, the lawyers critiqued her performance. Linda admitted getting caught up in the brouhaha, after all, this wasn't an easy task and part of her job. The staffers' critical mission was vital for the Clintons' political boom, and the politicals' continued employment. The anticipation of *Could we pull it off?* infected them all. Their mission didn't involve America's interest, but humanizing the First Lady, and maybe, just maybe, putting the Whitewater monster and co-president thing to bed.

Finally, the stage was set. A newly contrite Hillary in a pink sweater twin-set greeted the press. This was big news. All the major networks broke into their regular programming to air it live. "It was stagecraft and theatrics at its finest," Linda stated. With hair combed back, Hillary took a seat in the warmly lit beige and gold State Dining Room, as planned. She folded her hands nicely in her lap—as coached. And what did the public hear? "Exactly what was planned to hear," Linda observed.

Did Hillary clear up Whitewater questions then? No, and she never did. As noted in the *New York Times*, "[Hillary] tried to banish the public doubts ... that have seemed suspicious, inconsistent and protective by pleading that any mistakes ... were caused by ineptitude ...."

"This is really a result of our inexperience in Washington," a honey-tongued Hillary said.[251]

The press left empty-handed as Hillary graciously exited. Waiting in the wings an overjoyed lawyer hollered, "We nailed it!" Linda remembered. Hillary had successfully concealed the bone-cracking reputation she earned when the cameras were off. *Who was that woman?*

For Linda, Hillary's press conference was great theater, "only problem was that the American people believed this was genuine."

The Clintons' tactics of public relations disguised as news reminded me of the marketing tricks Hollywood uses to sell movie tickets. Think about all the thrilling, expertly edited movie trailers you've watched that enticed you to buy tickets. After watching the film, you realize all the best parts were in the trailer and the movie was just a crappy movie. When it comes to second-rate movies, Hollywood's marketing deceptions may waste a couple hours of consumer time and twelve dollars. In politics, Hollywood's deceptive politicians' marketing tricks can have far-reaching and lasting consequences for hundreds of millions of people. Rhetoric and stage craft are not substitutes for substance, truth, or honorable, selfless leadership.

While true heroes were replaced with celebrities, wrapping candidates for elected office in pretty, perfect, shiny pop-culture packages fast became the false idol worship of politics. Consider how Hillary and Obama were both presented in this clichéd script as brilliant intellectuals, superior leaders with big ideas and solutions. Year after year they were infused with awards, honorary degrees, and fluff media profiles."[252]

Cited by the *National Law Journal* twice as one of "the 100 most influential lawyers in America," and considered by many to be "the smartest woman in the world," Hillary's attempt to take over America's health care "Hillarycare" crashed and burned, and Democrats lost control of both houses of Congress.[253]

In Obama's Hollywood media iteration, he reached messianic heights; a man who stood above the world—"almost like God." "The smartest man in the world," Obama, a law professor and former *Harvard Law Review* president, received a Nobel Peace Prize—although no discernable accomplishment warranted it.[254] His takeover of America's healthcare, ObamaCare, faces constitutional challenges, and waivers have been granted to Obama supporters, including unions and corporations, while all other Americans are mandated to buy it.[255]

Hillary and Obama's Alinskyite training stressed: "It is not enough to persuade them of your competence, talents, and courage—they must have faith in your ability and courage. They must believe in your capacity not just to provide the opportunity for action, power, change, adventure ... but to give a very definite promise, almost an assurance of victory. They must also have faith in your courage to fight...."[256] Alinsky also instructs, "Since people understand only in terms of their own experience, an organizer must have at least a cursory familiarity with their experience."[257]

While campaigning in 2008, crafted as commander-in-chief, ready to lead on day one, Hillary repeatedly "misspoke" when she happily claimed that as First Lady she had dodged sniper fire in Bosnia as her credentials. A video of her supposed daredevil trip showing her being greeted by children with flowers blew up that deception.[258]

When Obama claimed his uncle was part of the American troops that liberated Auschwitz in World War II in 1945, the public was told that he, too, simply "misspoke." Obama's statement could have been true—had his uncle served in Joseph Stalin's Red Army.[259]

PR and showmanship trumped justice in the Clinton White House. The unholy alliance, the collusion of Hollywood make-believe tricks and politics, concealed the stubborn facts from the public view. Contrary to what the Clintons publicly contend or wrote in memoirs, in the unedited, unvarnished picture, they withheld documents, stonewalled subpoenas, and influenced testimony in the Travelgate, Whitewater, and Foster investigations.

———

That spring in 1994 was also the end of Linda's White House career. It started with a conversation she had with longtime Clinton confidante Bruce Lindsey, whom she considered a friend, and was described as "the first to see [Bill] in the morning and the last one to see him at night,"[260]

"Fear was my motivator. I was so tired of being afraid," she griped, and she was when she went to Lindsey. With the independent counsel reinstated, staffers were subpoenaed, and Linda was named a witness for Foster's death investigation and Whitewater. Whether she was growing paranoid or not, Linda felt that the Clintons' new politicals were shutting her out and wanted her out. She claimed to overhear troubling whispers like, "She's hearing too much ...."

"Look, I don't understand this," [she] said to Lindsey, "I've been loyal. I have worked through these horrible investigations ... I don't understand why all of a sudden I'm not considered of any value. What has changed?' And [Lindsey] said, 'Look, nothing's changed. You are valued....' My feeling was that for some reason I was not thought to be 'on the team,' which is a phrase you hear a lot and I had not at that point done anything not to be on the team."[261]

Lindsey apparently listened thoughtfully to her concerns when darkness flashed through his once-kind eyes. He fired a loaded phrase at her when he said, "Talk like that will get you destroyed." Linda's stomach sank to her knees.[262] She understood, quickly excusing herself.

In a whirlwind, quick intervention from top White House brass had Linda transferred to the Pentagon. The shock of being kicked out of the White House was devastating, especially since she had played by their rules during the investigations. She described how her banishment was in the form of "get her out quickly, but not angry." Instead of outright firing her, where she'd be perceived as hostile or a threat, perhaps angry enough to hurt the Clintons by being truthful on the witness stand, she got the "get her out wearing a smile" treatment. But there was a catch—a big one. Even as she was given a promotion to ease the heave ho, a heavy string was attached. Linda was stripped of her careerist civil servant protections and reassigned as a political appointee. She felt it was a protectionist tactic to keep her quiet, dependent, and under their control, especially as more subpoenas with her name on them rolled in. It worked.

Linda, who believed she would go on to work for several additional administrations, who had served as an apolitical for nearly two decades in government, now owed her job to a political party— the Democrats, and more specifically, the Clintons.

"I had no choice. The Clinton White House knew it and so did I. I needed the job and you better believe I played by their rules. Everybody else did," Linda said. "I also knew that a disparaging rumor from me and I'd be fired."

Finding herself with an atrocious decision for any single parent to have to make— provide for her family or face unemployment, Linda took the Pentagon post.

"If you're not loyal to them, the Clintons will construct a means of forcing your loyalty so you can feed your children," Linda said. "Once they've got you, it's impossible to extricate yourself from their clutches."

Linda kicked into survival mode. "All I could think about was 'work hard, keep my mouth shut, nothing bad will happen' and try to regain my careerist status."

She pacified herself with one consolation, however, she'd never have to deal with the two-faced Clintons again; the shiny PR-savvy faces the public knew, versus the ruthless faces behind the cameras she and her humiliated, subpoenaed, unemployed, indicted, or dead former colleagues knew. Never in a million years did Linda envision the Clintons giving her a second thought.

It was a bumpy ride to the Pentagon. When Linda arrived, the position she was offered, to support the Secretary of Defense, was filled. The lady who had it, a Clinton political appointee, didn't want or need support from Linda.

After more turbulence, she was moved into a deputy director position, taking on the role as Pentagon spokesperson for the Joint Civilian Orientation Conference. It was a position for which she had no prior experience, running a program that allowed prominent civilians to tour military installations. Rising to the challenge, Linda worked hard and earned high praise.

Kenneth Bacon, the assistant secretary of defense for public affairs, (and Monica Lewinsky's future boss), later acknowledged, "[Linda] has worked on that program and came in at a time when it was facing some challenges and helped resolve those challenges and has done a good job."[263] The Pentagon was very accommodating in her work schedule for her need to prepare for the Senate depositions on Whitewater.

Chapter 12: Pentagon: Dumping Ground for White House Misfits

"There is nothing concealed that will not be disclosed,
or hidden that will not be made known."

—Luke 12:2 (NIV)

When Monica Lewinsky, Bill's paramour, and subordinate government employee, was transferred to the Pentagon in April 1996, the White House staffers behind that decision—including Bill's Chief of Staff Leon Panetta, Monica's former boss; and Evelyn Lieberman, Hillary's deputy chief of staff, and her "eyes and ears"—could have placed Lewinsky anywhere in government, or even in any of the Pentagon's offices within its vast seventeen miles of corridors, making it a virtual impossibility for Monica and Linda to have met. Instead, the disgruntled former White House staffers were thrown into the same Pentagon suite. [264]

Leon Panetta later served as President Obama's head of the Central Intelligence Agency and heads the Department of Defense.[265] Evelyn Lieberman served as chief operating officer to Hillary's failed 2008 presidential bid. [266]

"How could anyone be surprised at the inevitable end result?" Linda rhetorically said.

Monica Lewinsky began interning at the White House in November 1995 when she was twenty-one years old. The daughter of divorced parents, an oncologist and socially determined housewife, Monica was raised in Beverly Hills, California. During a government shutdown, she brought pizza to President Clinton and flirted with him, igniting their eighteen-month consensual sexual relationship. Shortly after their first sexual encounter, Monica was promoted to a paid staff member.[267] The Clinton-Lewinsky sexual encounters kept people waiting, be it other White House staffers or world leaders. They occurred when President Clinton was on the phone with policy makers or advisers, and became part of Betty Currie's job responsibilities. (Currie was Clinton's personal secretary, whom Linda called a "facilitator.")[268] Although Hillary denied knowledge of Monica's relationship with her husband, Lieberman (whom Linda called a "protector") testified that "the president was vulnerable to these kind of rumors" [Clinton with other women] and she also acknowledged that "that was one of the reasons for moving Ms. Lewinsky" out of the White House.[269]

And Linda's belief? "Considering Hillary's cult of aides whose primary responsibilities were to ferret out her husband's misbehavior and to keep her informed, in all probability Hillary almost certainly knew all about Monica ... She had a lifetime of related experience to draw reasonable inferences ... She knew of a cadre of women 'working' at the White House who were similarly 'involved' with her husband. The staff knew. We didn't need our own secret police to tell us. It was kind of hard to miss. As long as it stayed quiet, she didn't appear to care much. She cared a great deal, however, that he not get caught."

Saul Alinsky noted, "I have not known really competent organizers who were concerned about celibacy. The commitment is to the 'work.'"[270]

Back at the Pentagon, Linda peripherally had heard of the "new girl" because of rumors percolating she was someone's pet rock. How else would such a young, inexperienced girl land the prestigious job of confidential assistant to the Assistant Secretary of Defense for Public Affairs Kenneth Bacon? Monica's position typically was filled by a person with years of executive experience and an impeccable and unblemished background because top security clearance was required. The job came with a good pay grade and international travel.

What Linda didn't know was that Monica had been kicked out of the White House to the Pentagon "wearing a smile," just like she'd been.[271]

This career advancement tactic appears in the Obama administration. In 2009, Van Jones, Obama's former Green Jobs Czar, resigned when, in part, his self-described communist views came to light. John Podesta, of the George Soros-funded Center for American Progress, and friend of the Clintons and Obamas, stepped up.[272] Now at the Center for American Progress, Van Jones launched the American Rebuild the Dream movement, a so-called "Progressive" Tea Party, recycling the "peace and property" mantra the Clintons used in the 1990s.[273]

Linda was working on a campaign for the president and her office was filled with jumbos—large format photographs of President Clinton with the troops—when Monica first stopped in her office. When she reached out for one of the jumbos, Linda noticed a sullen sadness behind her smile. She seemed lost, miserable. Looking wistfully at the president's photographs, a jolt of excitement burst through her, and she said, "I know that tie he's wearing!" [Monica used to buy President Clinton ties.] Then she said, "That's Bruce Lindsey."

"Yes, I worked with him at the White House," Linda answered.

"I used to work at the White House, too," Monica responded longingly. And so began their ill-fated friendship.

Although Linda had a daughter a few years younger than Monica, Monica latched onto her immediately, apparently yearning for any connection to the White House, ingratiating herself, desperate to know who Linda knew. She was needy and clingy, spending the spring to fall going on *ad nauseam* about diets and her crush on President Clinton, calling him "handsome," and later "the big creep."[274] And she was a "pest" Linda tolerated, she said, because of her obvious connections.

Attempting to break Monica's monotonous chatter, one day, Linda joked with her, "It's a good thing he doesn't know about your crush. Probably would have jumped you." And she meant it, but being "jumped" by President Clinton wasn't something she'd wish upon anybody. How was Linda supposed to know her joke was true?

On America's national security front, terrorists attacked the United States each year of the Clinton administration.[275] Since Monica's White House internship began, al Qaeda had bombed an American training camp in Riyadh, Saudi Arabia, killing five Americans and wounding sixty more in November 1995. On June 25, 1996, terrorists had attacked America at Dhahran, Saudi Arabia, when a booby-trapped truck loaded with explosives bombed the Khobar Towers murdering nineteen U.S. airmen.[276] In August 1996, Osama bin Laden issued a public fatwa "calling on Muslims to drive American soldiers out of Saudi Arabia ... while celebrating the Saudi attacks ...." Bin Laden highlighted, "the 1993 firefight in Somalia,"[277] where President Clinton pulled troops out of Somalia after the October 3, 1993, battle of Mogadishu after eighteen soldiers were killed and two Black Hawk helicopters were lost. Bin Laden later stated, "Our boys were shocked by the low morale of the American soldier and they realized that the American soldier was just a paper tiger."[278]

We pick up Linda's story now (passing by the weeks in which bin Laden repeated a lecture to al Qaeda followers on the need to cut off "the head of the snake [United States]," to where Monica told Linda about "the affair."[279] It was shortly after the Clintons celebrated their twenty-first wedding anniversary and President Clinton's reelection looked promising.

It was eight a.m. on a crisp autumn morning when an anxious Monica was pacing a groove into the concourse at the Pentagon Metro Entrance as Linda arrived for work. Carrying two Starbucks coffees, Monica passed one to her.

"Linda, I've got something to tell you. Come with me. Oh my God, it's important." Rushing her off to the Pentagon's largest cafeteria, also known as the Greasy Spoon, she shuttled Linda through the breakfast mob toward a corner table. Linda had never seen her so alive. This wasn't the Monica of the last six months.

"Can't this wait till later?" Linda asked. "I'm going to be late. The finance officer is meeting me—" About to burst, Monica wouldn't accept "later." The smell of hundreds of pounds of bacon and eggs filled the air when they sat down and Monica hunched over and blurted out. "I've been giving the president blow jobs for the last year." *What?* Linda wondered if she'd heard right.

"You're having an affair with the President of the United States? Are you serious?"

"Yes, Linda," Monica sputtered. "Yeah, I mean, now you know. I'll be going back to the White House any day and I thought you should know." Then Monica's tone dropped and became serious. "We had to keep our distance you know—'cause of the presidential campaign, and the meanies, but now it's almost over and there's no way in hell Bob Dole's gonna win." ("Meanies" were White House staffers who kept Monica and President Clinton apart.)[280]

And with that, Monica animatedly sat back, almost hitting the group of people eating breakfast behind them, and exclaimed, "The president promised me that as soon as the election was over he'd bring me back to the White House just like that." Snap! snapping her fingers high above her face. Instantly, Linda realized how and why she'd been kicked out of the White House. It all began to make a sickening sort of sense. "Don't look at me like that," Monica said.

"But, but, I thought ah, you—" Linda gasped, as a blur of Army green and Air Force blue milled around them, and the walls closed in. Then Monica spoke louder to compensate over the cafeteria chatter.

"He really wants me at the White House more than anything, Linda. Listen to me. You know, I mean, in just a few days after the election we can finally be together." Words stuck in Linda's throat. *She's got to be kidding.*

"Come on, Linda, what's your problem? Oh my God, there were like so many times I wanted to tell you. It's like, all those times when you said, 'It's a good thing he didn't know about my crush, 'cause he would've acted on it.' Oh my God, you don't know how many times I wanted to tell you. He did! He did!" Pushing her long black curls out of her face, Monica's guttural laugh seemed to rock the cafeteria. "Aren't you happy for me at least?" Wide-eyed, Monica rambled on, but disgust and outrage shut down Linda's hearing. Her knees buckled. The only good thing was she was sitting down.

The rumors alleging she was someone's pet rock were almost true but the hallway gossip had guessed wrong. Monica wasn't Ken Bacon's pet rock or some faceless White House staffer; she was President Clinton's.

How could I've been so stupid! Or was I purposely blind? Linda scolded herself. Yes, it was odd when Monica jetted off to New York City for President Clinton's Radio City fiftieth birthday party.[281] And there were all the times Monica had agonized over what to wear to various White House functions and State arrivals she'd attended. But who was she to tell Monica what to do? Rock stars have groupies, why not presidents?

Was it possible that President Clinton would have an affair with this young, immature, volatile girl? Impossible. Even for him. *She's got to be lying,* Linda rationalized. But she wasn't. "And I mean we have phone sex, too." Monica boasted with a wink. "I'll prove it to you. I'll page Betty now." Linda cringed.

It was awful. The ramifications were staggering, for Monica, for the president, but most of all for the country—and what about co-president Hillary?! Linda was at once furious, livid, nauseated, scared. *God help me! What has President Clinton done?*

The ring of Monica's cell phone brought Linda back to the present. It was President Clinton's personal secretary, Betty Currie. *What? So this is true?* Her fury shifted to resentment. *How could you tell me this? This—I don't need to know. You can't un-ring this bell.* This information would forever bind her to Monica and her dangerous liaison with the President of the United States.

"For God's sake Monica, you've got to end this immediately. This is nuts. You are one of a cast of thousands," Linda implored. "Are you crazy? He's using you."

"Oh my God, Linda, you don't understand," Monica dismissed. "It's like you just don't get it." Excited, Monica's voice raised again. Linda clenched her teeth. "When you know the whole story, you'll see I'm right. What's your number? I'll call you at home tonight and tell you everything."

"Monica you're not listening to me," Linda implored exasperatedly. "You can't be in love with him after giving him blow jobs. Don't you get it? You are disposable. You deserve more than being treated like some hooker. Please, you've got to end this. He's got a daughter about your age for God's sake."

But Linda's advice, as she recounted to me, fell upon deaf ears as Monica continued planning her future with Bill Clinton. But abruptly Linda's resentment quick-sanded to fear. "Have you ever done anything that could come back and hurt the president or the country?" Maureen's words to her the first day at the White House found a scary home in her mind.

When President Clinton first took office, Linda had had doubts whether or not he would pass an FBI clearance. Now they were confirmed.

The fact is, President Clinton violated his own Executive Order 12968 which reads in part: "In order for an individual to be eligible for access to classified material they must have a record of 'strength of character, trustworthiness, honesty, reliability, discretion and sound judgment, as well as freedom from conflicting allegiance and potential for coercion.'"[282] When it emerged that President Clinton "suspected that a foreign embassy was tapping his telephones and he proposed cover stories" if [Monica and he] were ever caught, he clearly knew the risks yet he continued the affair.[283] Monica could have blackmailed the president, but luckily she only wanted him or a job. Moreover, Linda and the other people Monica confided in also had leverage had they decided to wield it.

"Linda, Linda, when I'm with him, I've never been happier in my whole life. You should see us together. I mean, I know he's my soul mate." Monica chattered on, "Linda—hello! Why do you look like you're gonna pass out? Relax. You know, have some more coffee. Look, nobody knows except my mom and my aunt Debbie and they're totally cool—"

Just shut up, Monica! screamed in Linda's thoughts. *God help me. What's she gotten me into?* She couldn't escape the Clintons.

Chapter 13: Want to be Famous?

"You shall not go up and down as a dispenser of gossip and scandal among your people, nor shall you [secure yourself by false testimony or by silence and] endanger the life of your neighbor. I am the Lord."

—Leviticus 19:16 (AMP)

It was March 24, 1997, when a man with scruffy, tousled hair accosted Linda in her Pentagon office. "Linda Tripp," he said. Startled, she looked up from her desk.

"Hi. Mike Isikoff from *Newsweek*—remember?"

Yes, indeed. Linda knew exactly who he was from her Bush White House Media Affairs days and she also knew that Isikoff was not a reporter who gave up, ever. His notable investigative tenacity included breaking the news of televangelist Jim Bakker's affair.[284]

She was, however, very surprised to see him at her desk. How did he get into the Pentagon fortress, unescorted? Her defenses were up. She assumed he must want a scoop. Her role as the Pentagon spokesperson for the Joint Civilian Orientation Conference could be that scoop. It was after all "a multimillion-dollar taxpayer-funded boondoggle, a brainchild of the Clinton administration" that gave the rich and celebrities a chance to "experience the military" by jetting around on government aircraft and firing weapons. Already, she said there had been some media poking around into its debatable purpose.[285] How was Linda going to justify this boondoggle to a pit-bull who smelled a scam?

They went to the Pentagon alley to speak privately. When they got there, Isikoff said, "Kathleen Willey has named you as a contemporaneous corroborative witness for the sexual charges she's making against the President of the United States." [286]

What?! Linda was thrown way off kilter. Her mind raced to Monica's latest meltdown because Clinton didn't call her as expected. But, but Kathleen? How could she get the pressure away from Kathleen? *They will destroy her. She's gone through enough hell—none of which she deserved.* Linda didn't know what to say. She decided to stall, buy her time to think. "You're barking up the wrong tree," was all she could think of.

Immediately after Isikoff left, Linda, in petrified self-preservation mode, did what every good Clinton team player always does—tipped them off. She raced back to her desk, grabbed the phone, and dialed Clinton's trusted aide Bruce Lindsey to warn him. She left a message almost four years to the day since last setting foot in the White House, shortly after Lindsey had scared the hell out of her. *"Talk like that will get you destroyed."*

Oh no! Someone blew the whistle on *her.* Someone gave her name to Isikoff. Unable to reach Lindsey or his assistant, she paged him: "Important re: Isikoff and Willey." No response. Then she sent emails: "Urgent: Matter of Significant National Media Interest. Urgent! Please call." Nothing. She must have called seven or eight times.

Unbeknownst to Linda, she was the "enemy" apparently out to "take down President Clinton." She wished someone would've told her. Had she known, she would not have bothered to try and warn the White House.

That night, Linda called Kathleen Willey. They hadn't spoken in years. It was January 1993 when Linda met Kathleen at the White House's Correspondence Unit. A former flight attendant, she was volunteering at the Comment's Line hotline, and immediately stood out. "Although petite, she's very attractive, friendly," Linda recalled, "and under-utilized, gracious, and impeccably turned out in Chanel."

Married to Edward Willey, a major Democrat contributor to Clinton's 1992 campaign, the Willeys were a socially and politically prominent family. Chatting, the two ladies hit it off. "You should try to get a position working at the White House Social Office," Linda suggested to her.

Kathleen followed her advice. Shortly thereafter she was placed in the West Wing's Social Office, frequently visiting Linda when she worked in the counsel's office.

In late summer 1993, Kathleen confessed that her husband was having financial troubles and she was desperate for a paying job. Able to schedule a meeting with President Clinton to discuss obtaining a paid position, a hopeful Kathleen had told Linda, "I'll come by your office afterwards."

At approximately 3:30 p.m., November 29, 1993, Linda left her desk for a break. She ran into Kathleen walking out of the elevator heading for her office. Kathleen was disheveled, her hair askew, her make-up smeared, with red marks on her neck. Crimsoned face, she seemed flustered, overwhelmed.

"I need your lipstick," Kathleen said with a trembling voice. "I need to speak to you right away." Linda's concerns grew as she watched Kathleen struggle to collect herself. For privacy they went outside.

"Linda, he groped me," Kathleen blurted out. *What?* Kathleen's voice shook when she described her meeting with President Clinton. "I walked into the Oval Office. The president poured me a cup of coffee and showed off his campaign button collection. I started to explain how badly I needed a paying job, how Ed and I were having financial troubles. The president listened, but didn't seem to hear me. 'Please Mr. President, I'm at your mercy, I need your help.'" She recounted, catching her breath. "He apologized for my troubles and then out of nowhere, a sudden attack. He, he grabbed my hand with such force—he, he jammed it on his crotch. 'I've wanted to do this since I first saw you,' he said. Then he put his hands on my breast and started feeling me up. Then, then he rammed his tongue down my throat. I froze." Kathleen's posture recoiled as she relived the moment. A mortified Linda took her hand. President Clinton stands an overpowering foot taller than Kathleen, rendering her defenseless.

"Still, still, still—holding coffee cup," Kathleen stumbled, her voice breaking, "I didn't know what do, what to say, so I mumbled something about the First Lady, or someone walking in. The president told me, smugly, 'Don't worry, I've got that covered,'" in between ramming his tongue down her throat.

"I said, 'Stop! What if someone comes in? What about peep holes, cameras?' He said, 'Deny, deny, deny. This never happened. No one can prove a thing.' He was out of control, Linda. His veins popped out of his neck and forehead, his face flushed purple." (Bill used the same "deny" instructions with Gennifer Flowers, who'd had an affair with him in Arkansas, that was caught on tape: "I just think that if everybody's on record denying, you've got no problem. If everybody kinda hangs tough, they're just not going to do anything. They can't.")[287]

Dropping her head in her hands, Kathleen sobbed, "Thank God someone came in or I don't know what I would've done. This is enormous." [288]

A sick knot tied in Linda's stomach as she tried to calm Kathleen down, but she was inconsolable, muttering between gulping breaths and trembling.

"We didn't know what to do," Linda hopelessly exclaimed to me.

Do you push sexual assault from the President of the United States out of your mind and try to forget it? Face him? Slap him? What?

"Who do you tell to make sure this never happens again?" Linda said to me repeatedly when I asked her why they didn't come forward earlier.

"Come forward? Say what?" Linda snapped back. "I knew the Clintons would deny it and then destroy us." Looking back, Linda told me how she wished that she and Kathleen would've handled things differently. Nobody should be violated in such a despicable manner—by the president, by anyone.

When Kathleen went home that fateful day, she discovered her husband was missing. Earlier, he had been accused of embezzling approximately $274,000. Less than twenty-four hours later she learned he was dead of an apparent suicide.[289] Her world was in crisis. Desperate, Kathleen reached out to President Clinton again for a paying job, and wrote appreciative notes that the Clinton White House would later release to discredit her, as part of their stay-in-power "nuts and sluts" character assassination tactic.[290]

And Linda? She, like Kathleen, fell into a denial survival abyss having her own reasons to avoid a confrontation with the Clintons.

Those who doubted Kathleen's groping allegation against President Clinton should ask themselves, if it didn't happen, then why did President Clinton give her a paying job in the counsel's office? How did she end up, by explicit presidential appointment, serving as the only non-expert with a U.S. delegation to international conferences in Copenhagen and Jakarta? The director of the State Department Office of International Programs said at the time, he was "kind of surprised" to see Kathleen on the trip. "A good way to get yourself into a jam is to ask too many questions when someone comes from the White House."[291]

Could it be that Kathleen like Linda, Monica, and others received the "wearing a smile treatment" from the White House?

The Clintons' history of attempting to keep people silent is well documented, not exclusive to women, and includes Actress Elizabeth Ward Gracen. She claimed she had a long-ago fling with President Clinton, and came under IRS scrutiny just weeks after receiving a warning that she could be audited if she didn't keep quiet. "I was physically scared," she said, "… between the 'friendly' calls … telling me to get out of town for my own good and then talking about the smear tactics on the other. I got scared."[292] The Clinton-critical *The American Spectator* was burglarized three times and audited by the IRS. "The National Rifle Association, The Heritage Foundation, The *National Review,* Freedom Alliance, National Center for Public Policy Research, American Policy Center, American Cause, Citizens Against Government Waste, Citizens for Honest Government, Progress and Freedom Foundation, Concerned Women for America, and the San Diego Chapter of Christian Coalition," and *Fox News* host Bill O'Reilly were also among those audited by the IRS.[293]

History repeats itself. In 2011, the Obama Administration kicked up the IRS intimidation tactic, "harassment by regulation," by asking the Federal Communications Commission "to require groups that run political ads to disclose their high-dollar donors."[294]

But back in 1993 Linda couldn't absorb the unthinkable—President Clinton was a sexual predator. She rejected it; fell into safe, easier denial, and kept towing the line.

But now it was 1997. Someone had blown the whistle on Kathleen's assault to *Newsweek's* Isikoff, and Linda, who was minding her business, at work, who'd tucked away that awful day from her memory, was scared senseless.

"Urgent! Urgent!" she fired off another round of messages to warn the White House about Isikoff. Stuck in a quagmire, fear consumed her. She knew the Clintons whacked hard to hold onto power until everything would be Linda's fault. Then she'd be dumped into their fail-safe political enemy arena—and the country would buy it.

Frantic, Linda sat looking at her phone. No response; then finally a ring. Hopeful it was the White House, she looked at her caller ID. Ugh. It was Monica again. With elbows on her desk, she caught her head in her hands, letting the machine pick up.

What was she going to do now!?

And then it came to pass. All of Linda's efforts to self-preserve, keep her job, repair her battered conscience, avoid the Clintons, and regain her careerist status were for naught. And, there were none of Hillary's vast right-wing conspiracy players or Republican enemies around to help her out.

Chapter 14: Crosshairs

"When justice is done, it brings joy to the righteous
but terror to evildoers."

—**Proverbs** 21:15 (NIV)

When Linda told Monica about Isikoff's Pentagon visit Monica was mortified. "That can't come out, Linda," she said. But Monica's worries soon multiplied because on May 24 she was hysterical because President Clinton dumped her. "How could he have messed with me so cruelly?"[295] Monica later said.

Three days later, on May 27, 1997, the Supreme Court rejected President Clinton's bid for immunity from a civil suit while in office. *Jones v. Clinton* sexual harassment suit was on.

Tending to America's business, President Clinton used his precious and valuable Oval Office time to meet with the director of the CIA … no, oops, he met with his jilted paramour Monica to discuss Linda.

Here's what happened. On July 3 Monica had sent a letter to President Clinton rebuking him for not bringing her back to the White House. She reminded him how she had left like a good girl, and included a warning/threat that she might have to explain to her parents why, and asked for help finding a job. When Monica saw President Clinton the next day on July 4, he reprimanded her. "It's illegal to threaten the President of the United States," he warned.[296] After hugs and tears, when Monica was about to leave, she mentioned to Bill that *Newsweek* was working on a Kathleen Willey article and had approached one of her colleagues.[297]

On July 14, 1997, Betty Currie, Clinton's secretary, summoned Monica to meet with the president again. Monica called Linda to share her good fortune before making a beeline for the White House. "Betty called! The Big Creep [her nickname for Bill] wants to see me again."

In that July 14 meeting, a cold, distant, I-mean-business version of President Clinton emerged from the Oval to greet Monica, and she was scared.

"Almost without preamble, President Clinton asked Monica if the 'unnamed' woman in her office was Linda Tripp."[298] Then he interrogated her over what she knew about Kathleen and *Newsweek,* and denied doing anything wrong.

"It was an unusual meeting," Monica testified. President Clinton "asked me if the woman that I had mentioned ... was Linda Tripp ... He asked me if I trusted her, and I said yes ... [she] had tried to contact Bruce Lindsey and [he] didn't return her phone call. ... The president ... asked me if I would just try to see if she would call [Bruce] and so I said I would try."[299]

As Linda recalled, for the next two weeks Monica, the good little soldier and agent for the president, fiercely lobbied her, "Call Bruce. He's expecting your call." On and on; in Linda's office, on the phone, day and night, "Team player, save your job. You're a political appointee; you have to call Bruce."

Linda refused because her prior urgent messages had been ignored. Had Monica not been President Clinton's paramour, this episode would've been laughable, but she was, and Linda resented being caught in another Clinton mess. Then Monica's lobbying grew ominous, "They know where you live, Linda. Don't be stupid. Call Bruce." Meanwhile, President Clinton frequently checked in on Monica's progress. Monica testified telling the president, "I'm trying, but [Linda's] a proud woman." [300]

History repeats itself. In 2011, the Obama administration attempted to intimidate witnesses into not testifying before Congress in the gun-running operation investigation "Fast and Furious," where countless Mexicans and U.S. Border Patrol Agent Brian Terry have been murdered by weapons the Justice Department allowed into Mexico.[301]

And still Linda did nothing but worry. She took no notes and didn't record one conversation. She was appalled that President Clinton was using this young girl to threaten her over *his* actions. Now you know another tactic in the Clinton playbook—intimidation and threats.

———

It was late July in 1997, when, with a click on the mouse pad, Linda's private nightmare became public. Matt Drudge of the *Drudge Report* reported the Kathleen Willey story was about to break. A frazzled Monica cornered Linda in her Pentagon cubicle creating another scene for their already-suspicious co-workers to witness. She 'fessed up to her about the July 14 meeting. Stunned, Linda was terrified: *The President of the United States was having a meeting about me!?*

"The July 14 meeting was critical," Linda later testified, "[Monica] was summoned to the White House to discuss me and certain guidance was given to Monica on what she had to do, to get me to do certain things"—to coerce Linda to lie *about Kathleen.*[302]

"Now will you call Bruce?" Monica wailed.

But it was too late. Had Bruce called her back in March, maybe things would have been different. As a Clinton team player, Linda had tried, and failed miserably, to convince Isikoff to back off the story. So she did what she always did and was coached to do: narrowly tell the truth, protect the Clintons and *herself.*

That summer, Linda had met with Isikoff at her home, partly because he already knew about Linda's 1996 aborted book proposal, *Behind Closed Doors: What I Saw at the Clinton White House.*[303] It was a book she had seriously considered writing when she was convinced it was critical for Americans to know what their president and his un-elected wife were up to. There were chapters written on Clinton's other women in it

But by June 1996 Linda wasn't sleeping well. Her usual fears about losing her job overwhelmed her and she chickened out.[304] "What would I do for forever?" she said to me. After reading a draft of the book proposal that left her cold, Linda called the New York literary agent (she had met through a friend from the Bush I White House) who had introduced her telephonically to the writer. Upon hearing Linda's decision to pull out, the agent told her off, and slammed the phone in her ear.

Back at the Pentagon, Monica was breathing down Linda's neck. "Call Bruce. He will call you back in less than one minute. I promise."

Tired and scared, Linda backed down. She paged President Clinton's senior aide. Less than 30 seconds later Bruce Lindsey was on the horn. A composed Monica sat down sweetly, smug. "See, I told you."

Scooting Monica out of her office, Linda said to Bruce, "Apparently, you want to talk to me, but not at work. Let's talk tonight when I am home."

Dark thoughts reeled through her mind. Linda hadn't received a White House phone call since she last testified in Whitewater and Foster's death. By the time she arrived home she had two calls. When she dialed Lindsey back, he said in a lawyerly, I-mean-business tone, "Linda, I'm calling on behalf of the president," putting the fear of God in her while asking her how she was doing. He prefaced each sentence with, "The president wants you to know this never happened."

The situation was ugly. First, Lindsey denied receiving her urgent messages. Second, an alarming déjà vu; she'd heard those very words that were now being directed at her, directed at others when she served in the Clinton White House during the investigations and knew what that meant—*intimidation, cover-up.* "I'm calling on behalf of the president ..." from the president's lawyers to "I'm calling on behalf of the First Lady ..." from her former boss or Foster speaking for Hillary.

"It's too late now, Bruce," Linda told him, struggling to sound calm. "I tried to reach you when something could've been done."

Then, she said, the familiar Clinton damage control script—discredit and destroy the accuser—emerged from Lindsey's mouth that went something like this: "You and I both know that Kathleen is unstable and on medication. You know that. Don't you Linda! Do you hear me? She's a crackpot. Kathleen is out to get the president."

Linda didn't budge initially. She was freaking out inside when she mustered her strength, "Are you aware that the incident in question happened the same day her husband committed suicide?" Linda countered.

Next, he accusatorily asked her if she had leaked the story to *Newsweek* (neither Linda nor Kathleen was Isikoff's source), and said, "Would you agree in a conversation with Bob Bennett [Clinton's lawyer in the Jones case] that you could honestly say that Kathleen's unstable?" He wouldn't let up. Finally, Linda agreed. What else could she do? The line went dead.[305]

Linda dropped to her knees and prayed. *God help me, what am I going to do?* She couldn't escape the tyranny of the Clintons. Not a minute would pass without a foreboding thought. She was in the crosshairs of an enraged and vindictive President of the United States. Now she knew he was after her, and she knew the drill. If she didn't join their cohesive strategy to get back on team Clinton, she'd become their next target. Shades of Travelgate, Foster, and Whitewater revisited her.

Getting back on team Clinton could be accomplished by meeting with President Clinton's lawyer, Bob Bennett, where she assumed he would advise her to plead the fifth or sign an affidavit to protect his client (evidently making the mistake of believing his client). Advising witnesses to sign false affidavits, suborning perjury, is a law-breaking tactic the Clinton White House has used. Monica Lewinsky signed a false one.[306]

History repeats itself. In 2011, General William Shelton, the head of the Air Force Space Command, told House members that "the Obama administration pressured [him] to change his prepared testimony in a way that would favor a company funded by a major Democratic donor." And Solyndra officials, of the bankrupt solar panel company that received $525 million from the Obama regime, pled the Fifth when asked to testify."[307] Shortly thereafter, the Obama White House rejected subpoenas from a Congressional Subcommittee on Oversight and Investigations regarding Solyndra.

Kathleen later testified that Bennett told her to assert her Fifth Amendment rights rather than answer questions about President Clinton in the Jones case, "I felt like it was a threat coming from the president," she said. Two days before Kathleen's scheduled testimony, a man in a jogging suit approached her, naming her children, her pets, asking about her car tires, "Don't you get the message?"[308]

Although some staffers were saddled with high legal fees, Linda wasn't one of them. She told me her White House-appointed lawyer never billed her. She was not unique to this Clinton stay-in-power-tactic. Clinton Impeachment Chief Investigative Counsel David Schippers reported in his book *Sell Out* that Kathleen's lawyer was approached by one of the president's lawyers to represent her. She wouldn't need to worry about fees because "we will take care of that," her lawyer was told. [309]

The next day, Linda wrestled with her options and as usual elected to play along with the Clintons. She arranged another meeting with Isikoff, this time, at a hairdresser's. He arrived when she sat in the chair.

"I'm on my way to meet with Bennett," she whispered.

"Doesn't matter. We're going to run with it," Isikoff began. "Everything has checked out."

Oh no, she thought.

Racing home, Linda's nerves were fried and she called her White House-appointed lawyer for help. To his credit, as Linda told me, he advised her not to meet with Bennett because the damage was already done and she'd have to be "neutralized" because she had foolishly spoken to Isikoff.

Following his advice Linda canceled her appointment with Bennett. Her lawyer had to be her advocate, right? Besides, she didn't start this. She'd tried to warn the White House and had always been a Clinton team player and protected Hillary and Bill. As Linda later testified about her time serving in the Clinton White House, "In fact, I had done things by omission that I felt had been disloyal to the permanent staff because I had chosen to be loyal to the counsel's office and to the president." [310]

Chapter 15: Spotlight

"It is not good to be partial to the wicked and so
deprive the innocent of justice."

—**Proverbs 18:5 (NIV)**

It was August 1997 when Linda grabbed her kids for Ocean City, Maryland, to try to live a normal life. Failing wretchedly, her kids constantly asked her, "Mom, I heard you last night. Why were you crying?" She was crying with worry because she knew the *Newsweek* story on Kathleen Willey's sexual harassment allegations against President Clinton would break soon. And then it did break. And then the Clintons blamed Linda, just as she had feared and predicted.

Having dubbed the alleged presidential grope "preposterous," President Clinton's attorney, Robert Bennett, said, "I smell a rat here ... Linda Tripp is not to be believed." The media ran with it.[311] Even the *Tonight Show*'s Jay Leno joked that Linda was transferred to the Pentagon so she wouldn't have to observe so much sex in the White House.

In another fierce crisis-of-conscious-versus-employment battle, Linda had negotiated with the truth again. She elected to give Isikoff what she thought was an exculpatory statement for President Clinton by doing what she had always done: narrowly tell the truth, while protecting the Clintons and herself.

It backfired. She was quoted as saying she had run into Willey in the West Wing "disheveled." Her "face was red and her lipstick was off."

Willey told Linda how the president groped her but she did not seem appalled. "She was flustered, happy and joyful. ... This was not a case of harassment."[312]

Bennett's quote in *Newsweek*, essentially calling Linda a liar, boosted by the power of the White House, effectively destroyed her reputation.

The threat of retribution came to a head again. Linda served at the pleasure of President Clinton. She'd been publicly identified as someone with particulars about his sordid sex life. Paula Jones's lawyers were on the hunt, doing their job, subpoenaing anyone with such knowledge. That summer, Kathleen was subpoenaed; it seemed inevitable that Linda would be next.[313] Thanks to Monica, Linda knew about their tawdry affair, and that a simple open-ended question the Jones lawyers would ask about other women would put her in a courtroom face off with President Clinton.

Meanwhile, Linda left Kathleen to fend for herself as the Clinton spin machine went on the attack to undermine her credibility. *Not to speak is to speak, not to stand is to stand.* Eventually a publisher friend of the Clintons (who once lost a libel suit to a Hollywood Madame and had to admit under oath to cheating on his wife with hookers), alleged Kathleen wanted to write a book. It's a charge Kathleen vehemently denied. [314]

All the while, Monica still stood by Bill, and informed Linda repeatedly with variations of the following, "The president feels you've screwed him, and considers you an enemy. You're in danger professionally and personally. You've got to fix this. You can't contradict the President of the United States. You're not being a team player. I mean it, Linda, your only hope is going to Bob Bennett and redeem yourself. Tell him you can't recall the Kathleen Willey incident."

Tired and intimidated, Linda agreed to get back on team Clinton, and wrote a letter to *Newsweek* "full of half-truths and spin" (as she described it to me) that claimed she had been misquoted. *Newsweek* declined to publish it. [315]

Still no tapes.

———

With her life in utter chaos, Linda spent the fall agonizing over her lousy options. She was terrified of being subpoenaed, and afraid of the president and Hillary. As a federal employee she'd taken an oath to uphold the law and she *must* report corruption. But this was the Clinton White House; she would lose her job.

"Until you have people with unlimited resources, unlimited power, and a complete lack of scruples come after you, you can't know the terror it invokes," she genuinely explained to me.

How could she make this information public about Monica and keep out of it herself? She had no idea. She just knew she was finally committed to testifying truthfully and completely.

Caught in a political tug-of-war, partisans on both sides of the aisle got it wrong when they blamed or gave Linda credit for President Clinton's impeachment. As Linda explained, "Isikoff had set into motion what would alter the course of history, not me." She was swept up in it. Thanks to Monica Lewinsky, her role in what became the Clinton-Lewinsky scandal "is directly attributable to being the unfortunate recipient, once again, to burdensome information." And it was President Clinton's lawyer, Robert Bennett's, quote, "Linda Tripp is not to be believed," that was the impetus to persuade her to protect herself from any more Clinton coercion—and get proof.

But who could help her? She couldn't call the police or the FBI.

"*Ah, hi, excuse me, but the President of the United States is demanding I lie under oath for him...*"

She didn't have the guts to call a press conference, like Paula Jones did when she stood up to President Clinton and sued him for sexual harassment.[316] Linda knew that the insidious "any means to an end" corruption at the Clinton White House reached the highest levels of the Justice Department from the Whitewater investigations. Now, she imagined testifying truthfully, contradicting President Clinton and Monica, where she'd be painted a nut on top of a perjurer.

"Fear has been the prime motivator for everything I have done since I first began working for the Clinton administration in January 1993," Linda told me. And as she testified, "I knew I had to arm myself with records, because no one would believe it. And I still didn't make the decision until October ... In fact, I had never even thought about the independent counsel in my wildest dreams. My idea was I'm going to arm myself with records so when I'm ... under oath I can testify truthfully, not be set up in a perjury trap, and say, 'Fine. You think I'm committing perjury, here. Have a look.'[317] That's it."

It was the end of September when Linda called the one person she thought would know what to do. But the big problem was would that person, the literary agent from her aborted book deal, accept her call unless there was something in it for them, or would the agent tell her off and slam the phone in her ear again? Linda had no clue. As she said, "Absolutely, I believed after the aborted book, they wouldn't have taken my call if there was nothing in it for them. And I desperately needed help."

Desperate situations spawn desperate measures. That's when Linda categorically decided she'd dangle the idea of another publishing event to the agent when she called for help. It was that dangle, that false idea that she wanted to write a book that the Clinton supporters would seize as a weapon and use against her. As she testified, "I reiterate that there was no book proposal at that time, this is no book proposal now and this had nothing to do with a book proposal."[318]

The literary agent answered first ring, and eventually recommended she buy a tape recorder from Radio Shack to tape her phone calls with the former White House intern.

Finally Linda had a way to protect herself and not be walked into a perjury trap. Tape record. Thank God. Determined, she held firm to her resolve; at least she tried to. As Linda testified, "I felt that it was an insurance policy so that it would be more difficult for them to fire me because they didn't like what I was saying under oath."[319]

Now we see another tactic of how the Clintons stayed in power, retaliation: tell the truth in public or under oath, lose your job.

History repeats itself. In 2011, President Obama's Bureau of Alcohol, Tobacco and Firearms fired the ATF agent whistleblower Vince Cefalu after he spoke out about the "Fast and Furious" gun running operation.[320]

Linda's nerves were shot. Having never shopped at Radio Shack, she wanted to get this over with quickly. She grabbed her purse, jumped in her van, and drove to the nearest one, agonizing during the two-mile drive. Her deliberations went something like this: "Taping someone is sleazy. Protect yourself or no one will believe you. Lie under oath. Think about your children. Linda Tripp is not to be believed. Talk like that will get you destroyed. They know where you live. I'm doing this just in case. Like insurance ... Self-defense. I won't have to use the tapes. President Clinton will convince Hillary to let him settle with Paula Jones and give her something huge in return. Nobody will ever know."

The first time Linda pushed play and record on the Radio Shack tape recorder hooked up to her phone, her heart raced. *Monica can hear the recorder! I know it. She knows it.* Evidently not.

————

By December both Monica and Linda had been subpoenaed to testify in the Paula Jones case and Linda was shocked.[321] "I know I was definitely not the one who told Paula Jones's attorneys the name because when they finally did subpoena [Monica] I was appalled. I didn't know how they had gotten her name," she testified.[322]

Linda had spoken to the Paula Jones lawyers *after* they contacted her to find out if they would withdraw Linda's subpoena and agree to a private interview "minus the tapes and hopefully without Bob Bennett," about Kathleen Willey.

Meanwhile Monica was pressuring Linda to lie about her relationship with President Clinton as well, even attempting to bribe Linda to lie with money from a condominium she owned in Australia.[323]

And then Linda did what she had done in the previous Clinton investigations—she protected her job. Early January 1998, she gave the tapes she had recorded of her conversations with Monica Lewinsky to her White House-appointed lawyer, to, as she testified, "do nothing but retain them and have custody of them." [324] "It never occurred to me that the tapes would become public. I thought they would be an insurance policy."[325]

After the Office of the Independent Counsel was made aware of Linda and her tapes via friends and associates of the Paula Jones camp, and she received an urgent telephone message to call the OIC "because they can't call you," a whistleblowing train flew down the fast track, but it was another one that Linda didn't drive. If she didn't contact the OIC she could be charged with withholding evidence. At that point, Linda knew she "was either with them [OIC] as their witness," or she was out there on her own with a president determined to get her back on team Clinton.[326]

"Had I known we'd be sitting here today, I promise you I would have done a better job," she testified before the grand jury. "It wasn't my idea that [the tapes] would be evidence in a case like this; it was to ensure that I was not convicted of perjury." [327]

Frantic Linda was beside herself when she went to retrieve her tapes, and discovered her White House-appointed lawyer was having them transcribed. "And it upset me that he did not turn them over immediately because of my concern that he, he may have been providing that information to the White House."[328] She fired him as soon as she got her tapes back.

Before Linda agreed to become a *reluctant* witness for Ken Starr's OIC and was granted federal immunity—what she called her "colossal error"—she repeatedly asked her new, temporary lawyer (whom she fired when she was convinced he had a political agenda and his advice did not reflect her best interests), if she should plead the fifth.

"Don't be ridiculous. Absolutely not," her counsel instructed her she said.

"I was assured and reassured that taping in Maryland was a non-issue. I had put my life in his hands, heeded his expert advice and waived my Fifth Amendment rights. It cost me dearly. Just ask the Maryland prosecutors," she said, shaking her head, when we spoke about his short tenure. "It was so crazy. I was in the middle of s–t storm with the White House. I didn't have time to shop for a lawyer." Then she directed her lawyer "to get her out of being deposed and off [Paula Jones's lawyers'] radar screen." As a federal witness, Linda did what was asked of her to fulfill her obligations under Ken Starr's OIC's federal immunity agreement.[329]

Chapter 16: Politics of Personal Destruction

"For the time is coming when [people] will not tolerate (endure) sound and wholesome instruction, but, having ears itching [for something pleasing and gratifying], they will gather to themselves one teacher after another to a considerable number, choosing to satisfy their own liking and to foster the errors they hold, and will turn aside from hearing the truth and wander off into myths and man-made fictions."

—2 Timothy 4:3-4 (AMP)

On January 26, 1998, six days after the Clinton-Lewinsky scandal broke, *some* truth about their affair had trickled out in the press, but to Linda it felt like eternity. That week, the "If the allegations are true, will Bill Clinton resign?" speculation percolated. The words "impeachment," "sex," "suborning perjury," "witness tampering," and "obstruction of justice" became talk show staples. The administration circled the wagons. The vigorous defense of President Clinton began.

The late lion of the Senate, Edward "Ted" Kennedy from Massachusetts, who in 2008 would dump Hillary, throwing his "Camelot" support behind Barack Obama for president, said, "[President Clinton] denied these allegations ... I believe that he'll be vindicated." [330] Secretary of State Madeleine Albright said she believed the allegations against Clinton were "completely untrue." Clinton Commerce Secretary William Daley, who was appointed

President Obama's second chief of staff in 2011, added, "I'll second that. Definitely." [331] Senior policy advisor Rahm Emanuel, President Obama's first chief of staff, dashed resignation talks and said, "Did the president have a sexual relationship with this young lady? No. Did the president ask this young lady to lie? No."[332] *CNN* analyst James Carville, die-hard Clinton defender, announced, "There's going to be a war ..." and the war was "between the friends of the president and the independent counsel."[333]

History repeats itself. Another political war. In 2011 Teamsters boss Jimmy Hoffa declared war with the Tea Party, "President Obama, this is your army. We are ready to march ... Let's take these sons of bitches out ...."[334] Next, President Obama and Democratic leaders like Bill Clinton, who defamed the Tea Party, spoke favorably about the "Occupy Wall Street" protests spreading across America and the world riddled with Marxists, communists, and socialists' protestors and supporters.[335]

President Clinton didn't correct anyone. As Linda knew, the Clintons had no shame; staffers, elected officials, anyone, could be used to lie to protect them.

And Linda? She was holed up in her safe house under protective guard with two new temporary lawyers. With the drapes pulled shut, in a frenzied pace, they were documenting how President Clinton attempted to fix the Paula Jones sexual harassment case.

Later that day in the White House Roosevelt Room, President Clinton, flanked by Hillary and Vice President Al Gore, wagged his finger in the world's face, and repeated his original denial of the allegations Linda captured accurately on tape: "I want to say one thing to the American people. I want you to listen to me. I'm not going to say this again. I did not have sexual relations with that woman, Miss Lewinsky. I never told anyone to lie, not a single time, never. These allegations are false and I need to go back to work for the American people." [336]

The nation sighed in collective relief. Who didn't want to believe their president? But not Linda, she had to remind herself to breath because she knew President Clinton was open to blackmail. He was lying, and Lewinsky had signed a false affidavit at his behest.[337]

It was unbelievable. Only days earlier, Linda had been threatened over Kathleen Willey. Now, the pressure was doubled. The stakes were higher for Linda to commit not one felony, but two because Monica needed to be covered-up as well.

Much of the narrative from Clinton supporters and an ideologically complicit media centered on the false accusation that Linda conspired to entrap President Clinton, but who was entrapping whom? Who conspired against the other using taxpayer-salaried staffers to solicit them to commit not one, but two crimes?

On June 22, 2004, President Bill Clinton told Oprah Winfrey: "So [the Republicans] were desperate, and you know, when Linda Tripp showed up, they all thought they'd died and gone to heaven." Who was desperate?[338]

The ease of President Clinton's angry denial scared Linda senseless. The insanity boggled the mind: "... never told anybody to lie." *Yeah, right.* Linda searched the TV screen for Harry Thomason or his wife. She knew the Hollywood image makers had to be lurking somewhere. She was right. Thomason arrived at the White House four days earlier to do what he did best: produce fictional Emmy award-winning television.[339]

After President Clinton's second denial, Hillary left, apparently satisfied with her husband's "latest untruth," and flew to New York, safe in the Secret Service's arms, to visit a Harlem school where she discussed values: honesty, caring, respect, and responsibility, and later dined at a UNICEF dinner.[340] There was no such fun on the horizon for Linda. She continued detailing the particulars of obstruction of justice in her hotel room safe house.

"My lawyers kept at me, 'I know you're tired, but we've got to finish.'" Linda recalled, "But I kept thinking, how do I explain the last two years in hours?" The OIC needed the sequence of the cover-up, from President Clinton to Bruce Lindsey on down to Monica. "Monica played a pivotal role in assisting the White House in the cover up. She initiated the conversations. She placed ninety-nine percent of the calls to me." Finally, nearing midnight, her bleary-eyed lawyers left.

Meanwhile, near 5:30 a.m., a limousine pulled up to New York City's magnificent Waldorf Astoria Hotel. Hillary, wearing a pink coat and fashioning a demure First Lady look, accompanied by her chief of staff, climbed in. Together, they rode through a squadron of media to the *NBC Studios* at Rockefeller Center, as the nation eagerly waited for her reaction. "I knew what was coming and dreaded all of it," Linda remembered.

What she dreaded was called the four Ds; deny, deceive, discredit and destroy—a tried-and-tested strategy the Clintons had discharged during previous investigations to stay in power. Change the dialogue, move culpability away from you, point the finger of guilt off of you, and blame someone else—usually the accuser.

When Hillary took her seat opposite Matt Lauer on NBC's *Today Show*, Linda's defenses were up. For the next eighteen minutes, it felt like an invisible hand was punching her stomach—hard.

First, Hillary dodged Lauer's question about the exact nature of her husband's relationship with Monica. Hillary said, "I think as this matter unfolds, the entire country will have more information ... the best thing to do in these cases is just to be patient, take a deep breath, and the truth will come out." Lauer persisted for an answer, when finally Hillary said, "The president has denied these allegations on all counts, unequivocally." There it is: *Deny.*

Hillary continued, "Bill and I have been accused of everything, including murder by some of the very same people who are behind these allegations ... this is part of the continuing political campaign against my husband." *Discredit* and blame the accusers.

Then Lauer solicited her opinion about special prosecutor Ken Starr when Hillary said, "We get a politically motivated prosecutor who is allied with the right-wing opponents of my husband." *Discredit.* Starr was doing his job.

"[He] spent $30 million," Lauer interjected.

"More than that now," Hillary said. Here, Hillary was telling the truth. The probes cost taxpayers over $60 million dollars and secured over 33 indictments.

"We're talking about Kenneth Starr," Lauer continued, "use his name ..."

"But it's the whole operation," Hillary claimed. "It's not just one person. It's an entire operation." *Deceive.* Linda had a reason to want an insurance policy if she told the truth.

And so forth. During Hillary's interview, deceptive and discrediting statements flowed freely and included:

- "It's just a very unfortunate turn of events that we are using the criminal justice system to try to achieve political ends in this country ..."
- "And I also believe that it's part of an effort, very frankly, to undo the results of two elections."
- "I do believe that this is a battle ... Look at the very people who are involved in this, they have popped up in other settings." In Linda's defense, she popped up because she worked at the Clinton White House and was subpoenaed.

Afterwards Hillary fired up the media, propelling them on a wild goose chase when she said: "This is the great story here for anybody willing to find it and write about it and explain it, is this vast right-wing conspiracy that has been conspiring against my husband since the day he announced for president. A few journalists have kind of caught on to it and explained it, but it has not yet been fully revealed to the American public."

To conclude, Hillary put the participants on notice, "And I think when all of this is put into context, and we really look at the people involved here, look at their motivations, look at their backgrounds, look at their past behavior, *some folks are going to have a lot to answer for* [Emphasis mine]."[341] There it is. The final D—*Destroy.*

And answer these Americans did. Linda, Ken Starr, the Office of Independent Counsel, and anyone involved directly or indirectly with the Paula Jones case was smeared and vilified until the truth came out and Hillary's husband was disbarred for five years and fined—after making a deal with the OIC's special prosecutor.[342]

Linda was correct. Hillary masterfully executed the Four D strategy. The latest Clinton damage-control script, their cohesive strategy, was complete: Linda+OIC+VRWC=bad/villain. Clintons=good/victim. Now we see another Clinton playbook tactic on how they stayed in power: the Four Ds. Hillary's *Today Show* appearance was impressive, but it wouldn't survive reality.

Saul Alinsky drilled: "The job... is getting the people to move, to act, to participate ... to develop and harness the necessary power to effectively conflict with the prevailing patterns and change them ... your function—to agitate to the point of conflict."[343]

Panic-stricken, Linda's head bobbed back as if pushed when Hillary said *"Some folks are going to have a lot to answer for,"* at what she perceived was a direct threat from Hillary and an ominous warning.

"I knew Hillary was talking about me," Linda said. "I knew the Clintons had to discredit me." She knew she had to be "neutralized" and destroyed like others before her. In less than twenty minutes, Linda was outgunned by the most powerful couple in the world.

The media pounced. Clinton supporters rallied. Now accusations that Bill was set up by a vast right-wing conspiracy were taking hold.

As Linda predicted, the character assassination phase in the Clinton self-preservation script rolled out. As *Newsweek* reported, "The Clinton camp began 'blast-faxing' journalists with an eleven-page, single-spaced 'fact sheet' weaving together a web of right-wing, Clinton-hating lawyers, with Linda Tripp in the middle like some kind of predatory spider ... (#11. Tripp Thought by Neighbors to Be a Republican)."[344]

Saul Alinsky's thirteenth rule: "Pick the target, freeze it, personalize it, and polarize it.... When you 'freeze the target,' you disregard these [rational but distracting] arguments and carry out your attack." [345]

Out came the Clintons' dirt-digging private investigators including Anthony Pellicano to investigate and sow villainous seeds of doubts. (In 2008, Pellicano, who wiretapped, followed, and intimidated people, was found guilty of 76 federal criminal charges for providing similar services in Los Angeles.)[346] Swiftly ex-spouses and schoolmates were hunted down. Linda's confidential FBI file was illegally leaked, violating the 1974 Privacy Act, by Clinton-appointed Pentagon officials, to *The New Yorker*, misrepresenting a teenage accusation of theft (charges were dismissed) as an arrest. The article accused Linda of lying about whether she had been arrested in a 1987 security-clearance form.[347] The 1974 Privacy Act "prohibits the government from releasing unauthorized personal information about individual Americans to nonfederal organization."[348] That leak sparked another taxpayer-funded investigation and more hell for Linda.[349] Everything and anything to discredit and destroy the Clintons' so-called political enemies was fair game.

History repeats itself. Obama's presidential re-election campaign launched a dirt-digging mission to damage potential opponents, including New Jersey Governor Chris Christie.[350]

Next, the idea that Linda was contemplating writing a book made big news and propagated the myth that this was all about a book.[351]

Meanwhile, less than four weeks after Hillary's *Today Show* appearance, on the national security front, deadly threats against America intensified. America's enemy, Osama bin Laden, issued a fatwa (his second) in his war against the "infidels." On February 23, 1998, the terror mastermind declared: "The ruling to kill the Americans and their allies—civilians and military—is an individual duty for every Muslim."[352]

But hey, sex sells, not jihad against the West.

Back in-country, the Clintons' political war against their American "enemies" consumed the media, virtually splitting the nation in two. It was divide-and-conquer politics where half the country condemned the right while the other side pointed towards the liberal left. Citizens were pitted against citizens. Friends became bitter foes. The media didn't always report the battle; they engaged in battle and, as a devoted mob, blindly jumped on Hillary's vast right-wing conspiracy bandwagon. Even NOW, the National Organization for Women, the largest feminist U.S. group, sided with President Clinton—not the women the Clintons attacked.[353]

Condemned as the "most reviled" and "hated woman in America" for "betraying" Monica, some days Linda felt as if the entire world hated her.[354] For seven distracting, circus-like, anti-Linda-mania months, her motive for "conspiring" to take down Bill Clinton boiled down to a grab-bag of reasons—from her alleged desire for fame, money, and a book deal to a near pathological hatred of the Clintons.[355]

And if those weren't enough reasons to despise her, the final shin kicker arrived with criticism of her physical appearance to certify her pariah status. The White House defined Linda, Hillary's VRWC, and Ken Starr's OIC with ferocious, partisan sex-crazed precision in a tidy worldwide squall of contempt

As Linda described it, "In lock step, with their three talking points memorized, polished Clinton communicators with appalling and awesome force bombarded a nation into believing that white was black; that the underlying criminal behavior was inconsequential in comparison to the despicable 'overweight' Linda Tripp agenda. And that the independent counsel, who was merely doing his job, was an out-of-control prosecutor with a sick sense of puritanical self-righteousness—also out to get the president." [356]

The Clintons' epic blame-and-destroy their political enemies strategy, which brought victory to them in the past, was within their reach until Jury Exhibit BC2-11 in Ken Starr's investigation—forensic evidence—stopped them. It was Monica's now-infamous blue Gap Dress which was walloped with President Clinton's semen during one of their White House rendezvous.

In 2011, former New York Congressman Anthony Weiner, married to Hillary's deputy chief of staff, Huma Abedin, used this "blame-and-destroy" tactic when he was caught sending lewd pictures of himself to young women over the Internet and tried to pin it on innocent people (Andrew Breitbart and fictitious hackers).[357]

Did Linda encourage Monica to keep the dress? Absolutely. She thanked God for the dress. The thought of Monica dry-cleaning it in the event President Clinton lied (he did) made her want to scream. Knowing of its existence provided her with a tad of hope that maybe, just maybe, this time the Clintons' lies would be exposed.

As Linda armed herself with proof, she begged Monica to do the same.[358] It was prophetic advice considering the Clinton White House began a devastating whispering campaign that the overweight Monica was "unstable," and "was known in the West Wing as 'the stalker'" to discredit and destroy her.[359]

And Hillary?

One has to wonder if her chilling indifference to the lives of these women whom her husband exploited had a coarsening effect on her. Did it lower her threshold of sympathy, permit her to hurt innocents and even encourage deterioration in society because Hillary, cloaked in a do-good wrapping, helped attack Monica? As a senior White House aide testified, Hillary was "distressed" her husband was being attacked, for political reasons, for "his ministry of a troubled person."[360]

On Linda's third day of testifying in Ken Starr's grand jury as a federal witness in the Clinton-Lewinsky investigation, Maryland's State Attorney opened up a probe to decide whether or not to criminally prosecute her for taping her conversations with Monica Lewinsky.[361] Already survival-weary since President Clinton's winter denials, Hillary's vast right-wing conspiracy charge, death threats, her safe house sojourn, and having morphed into a human piñata eviscerated in the press, Linda's summer of 1998 brought forth horrific worries of sitting behind vertical bars when she took her seat to testify.

Was the Maryland state prosecutor's announcement an attempt to remind Linda to color her testimony or develop amnesia as other Clinton staffers had experienced? She certainly suspected so and viewed the indictment threat as a scare tactic by using the justice system for political gain.

History repeats itself. ACORN, the Association of Community Organizations for Reform Now, filed a lawsuit against James O'Keefe, Hannah Giles, and Breitbart.com LLC for what it alleged was illegal videotaping of ACORN employees in Maryland.[362]

The media talking head consensus was assorted but tilting against her. A greatest-hits selection of reasons why she deserved to be indicted was because Linda's actions were deplorable: she dared to conspire against the Clintons, she betrayed her "friend" Monica, or she knew it was illegal to tape and still did it. [363]

"If it's against the law, why do they sell taping devises in Maryland?" Linda said to me.

Looking back, had she conspired to bring down President Clinton, and known the Maryland two-party taping laws, she would've planned better and made different choices. First, she would've taped Monica when she was in Virginia at work or travelling when Monica called from her D.C. apartment. And, secondly she would've asked specific questions, kept the receipts for the tapes and batteries, and labeled every audio tape to hand over to investigators who needed such evidence, instead of turning her house upside down to ensure she had given them all of the original tapes.

Meanwhile, on the national security front a month later, on August 7, 1998, al Qaeda terrorists struck the United States, bombing U.S. embassies in Kenya and Tanzania minutes apart, killing over 200 people, including twelve Americans.[364] Next up in the United States, Monica Lewinsky is slated to testify in the Clinton-Lewinsky scandal.

Chapter 17: Oops

Days later on August 17, 1998, seven brutal months after the Clinton-Lewinsky scandal broke, in a televised address, President Bill Clinton had something to tell America: "Indeed, I did have a relationship with Miss Lewinsky that was not appropriate. In fact, it was wrong," he glumly said. "It constituted a critical lapse in judgment and a personal failure on my part for which I am solely and completely responsible." [365]

Oops.

Ken Starr submitted his Office of the Independent Counsel report to Congress that September, citing eleven impeachable offenses against President Clinton. Seventy-eight newspapers called on him to resign. The *New York Times* and *Washington Post* "denounced his conduct ... but stopped short of calling for his resignation or impeachment." [366] Around the globe, "international papers expressed deep concern over the turmoil in Washington and its possible impact on the stability of U.S. global leadership." [367]

The nation the Founding Fathers created, rooted in Judeo-Christian beliefs, was scandal-ridden, mired in deception and immorality.

Had President Clinton told the truth and not tried to dodge a perjury charge by claiming oral sex wasn't really sex, his legacy might not include the "Clinton-Lewinsky Effect" where sex researchers found that college students are "growing more hesitant to call oral sex actual sex."[368]

Had Bill Clinton told the truth, perhaps the world might've been spared this "gross-out" from Monica's testimony where she described masturbating with a cigar just off the Oval Office while he masturbated and watched. [369]

Likewise, had it not been for his intransigence, the mainstreaming of "blow jobs" and other taboo, unhealthy sexual activities into the national dialogue ("Blow Jobs Are the New Goodnight Kiss") might not have become a disturbing growing teen trend.[370]

Post Clinton-Lewinsky, oral sex is now the main cause of oral cancer and there's an uptick in syphilis and gonorrhea of the mouth.[371] According to the Justice Department, one in five women will be sexually assaulted or raped while in college. Victims groups say colleges may be putting their finances and images before the victims, by blaming the victim while protecting the accused.[372] Sound familiar?

President Clinton degraded the presidency. When Juanita Broaddrick's credible rape allegation against him emerged in January 1999, Clinton defenders still blindly rallied behind him.[373] This was even after Broaddrick disclosed Hillary's help in covering it up when Hillary approached her at a political rally and coldly said: "We want to thank you for everything you do for Bill." Hillary had kept a tight grip on Broaddrick's hand, drawn her closer, and repeated her statement, but with a coldness and look of intimidation that was unmistakable.[374] Hillary never answered questions about these serious charges or her potential role in covering them up. Notice how the media failed to bring up any of this when she ran for President in 2008.

Instead the Clintons continue to proclaim themselves advocates for women and children. Hillary's crowd-pleasing mantra is she will "fight for you" (unless you are Paula Jones, Kathleen Willey, Linda Tripp, Juanita Broderick, Monica Lewinsky, law enforcement doing your job, or people of different political persuasions).[375] As President Obama's Secretary of State, Hillary tells women in the Middle East, "We see women and girls across the world who are oppressed and violated and demeaned and degraded and denied so much of what they are entitled to as our fellow human beings." But if her husband violates you and he abuses his power, Hillary will help him destroy you.

President Clinton was impeached in the House of Representative and acquitted in the Senate.[376] Instead of keeping true to the principals of truth and justice and holding a president who abused his power accountable, Senate Republicans and Democrats caved in to public opinion, and to the Clintons' revised "It-was-all-about-sex" public relations production.

The year of Clinton and Lewinsky was a blight on America's prestige. It made a mockery of the rule of law. The leader of the free world, who put America's national security at risk over blow jobs, was a laughing stock. Instead of obeying his oath to protect and defend the Constitution, President Clinton with the help of Hillary used the White House to protect and defend both of them yet again.

Under Hillary's watch as President Obama's secretary of state, America's prestige continued to plummet. The biggest breach to America's national security occurred when WikiLeaks leaked hundreds of thousands of State Department cables on the Internet, damaging U.S. diplomacy efforts worldwide and endangering countless lives. As of this writing no senior official has been held to account.[377]

Bill Clinton later explained his conduct with Monica this way: "I have found this whole parallel lives theme … that whenever I was angry or under great stress, I was more likely to make a mistake, to run back into the dark alley of my parallel lives."

As Juanita Brodderick recounted her brutal rape: Bill "was such a different person at that moment, he was just a vicious awful person." [378]

Misunderstandings come in two forms. The first is when people are unable to intellectually grasp the facts. Secondly, is when people refuse to see it; rejecting what is clearly in front of them because they have no interest in the truth or it is not in *their* best interest to acknowledge it.

And Linda? When the truth came out, that yes, yes! she had made the tapes for insurance purposes only, that she did not work in cahoots with Hillary's so-called vast right-wing conspiracy, the damage was already done. By then the country had tuned out.

Linda was neither the whistle-blowing hero the right embraced nor the villain the left reviled—but she was used as such for political purposes by both sides. The truth was in the middle. Her speech on the courthouse steps after she testified in Starr's grand jury summed it up best: "I understand that there's been a great deal of speculation about just who I am and how I got here. Well, the answer is simple. I'm you. I'm just like you. I'm an average American who found herself in a situation not of her own making."[379]

As Linda frequently admitted to me, "I was gutless. I didn't want to lose my job. I didn't want to have something horrible happen."[380]

Although Linda had been vindicated by President Clinton's forced truth telling, it didn't improve her public image. She remained toxic, radioactive, marginalized, with no hope of redemption because as the Clintons' rewritten cohesive strategy declared, what President Clinton did paled in comparison to her actions. It was all about sex, and their sex-crazed political enemies poking into a personal issue, instead of witness tampering, obstruction of justice, and suborning perjury.

Saul Alinsky's fourth rule: "Make the enemy live up to their own book of rules. You can kill them with this, for they can no more obey their own rules than the Christian church can live up to Christianity."[381]

Twenty-four hours before President Clinton's last day in the White House, he struck a deal with independent counsel Robert W. Ray (who succeeded Ken Starr). President Clinton gave up his Arkansas law license for five years and acknowledged giving false testimony under oath .... And he was freed "from the shadow of both a possible criminal indictment and a continued fight with Arkansas court officials over their efforts to permanently disbar him."[382]

The fish rots from the head down.

From Whitewater to blow jobs to terrorism and beyond, the Clintons used the same strategies and tactics to stay in power—to reemerge on the world stage and in the Obama Administration.

Even with the Clintons out of the White House, the evidence withholding and destruction tactic continues to be in effect. This time it was during the 9/11 Commission investigation into the September 11, 2001, terrorists attacks, and it occurred in plain sight. In 2005, former Clinton National Security Advisor Sandy Berger was caught red handed "taking classified documents [related to the 9/11 commission investigations] from the National Archives and cutting them up with scissors."[383] "In his plea, Berger also admitted that he concealed and removed his handwritten notes from the Archives prior to a classification review."[384]

Let's look at the facts. Robert Ray *declined* to prosecute Bill Clinton during the Clinton-Lewinsky investigation although he *could have*, just like other special prosecutors could've prosecuted Hillary and Bill Clinton in earlier investigations for being "factually incorrect" and "withholding evidence." [385] As the OIC's final report states: "The Independent Counsel concluded that sufficient evidence existed to prosecute and that such evidence would 'probably be sufficient to obtain and sustain a conviction ... by an unbiased trier of fact.'"[386]

Ask yourself once again, no matter where your political ideology falls, would you have walked away free with a slap on the wrist had you done any of that?

Chapter 18: Free?

The Clinton White House saga doesn't end here because long-term power aspirations depend on maintaining the illusion. President Clinton, while promoting his book with Oprah Winfrey, said, "... the only reason the [Clinton-Lewinsky scandal] ever came out is because of the frustration my adversaries had that Kenneth Starr's investigations had produced nothing."

Oprah: "Well, we all think it came out because of Linda Tripp."

Bill Clinton: "It did come out because of Linda Tripp.[387]

No, it didn't come out because of Linda Tripp. The Clintons know that, and so does Linda's lawyer, yes, her lawyer—even as Team Tripp fundraised using that false "whistleblower" platform (probably because fundraising with Linda as a non-whistleblower wouldn't be as lucrative).

Switch gears as we jump to May 24, 2000, to when Linda's Maryland criminal wiretapping charges are dropped, a year and two months after she was indicted.[388] They were dropped due to insufficient evidence, and the pesky fact that the prosecution's main witness, Lewinsky, was not credible. She had lied in a sworn affidavit to protect Bill.[389]

Hallelujah!

After "six years of oppression, fear, and terror at the hands of these criminals" as Linda referred to the Clintons, she was able to say, "I finally have control of my life. Here's what happened inside the White House. I'm coming clean." But that would have to wait. Because despite being staked out by the press, Linda didn't appear publicly when her charges were dropped as she was recovering from nine hours of reconstructive plastic surgery.[390] Instead she issued a statement, via her lawyer, that read in part: "I was given federal immunity when I brought forward evidence that proved the President of the United States actively tried to fix a court case and that I was pressured to do the same … With God's blessings and the help of hundreds and thousands of supporters … I will continue to fight the shameful smear tactics of this corrupt administration."[391]

I hadn't seen Linda in weeks. I'd encountered so many false starts with her about writing her story that I'd pretty much given up hope and taken on another assignment. Her second surgery was news to me. But I did call to congratulate her. The response she was receiving was overwhelming. Thousands of well wishes poured into her website.

"I've had everything from marriage proposals to telling me I'm the equivalent of Rosa Parks to encouragement to run for the House of Representatives," she told me, obviously elated, relieved. Among those who sent congratulatory emails was Johnny Chung (from Chinagate fame, the Clinton White House 1996 campaign finance scandal).[392] He wrote how after three years of fighting the White House, he understood what she's gone through. Others wrote to tell her about the silent majority of Americans who were behind her. Now, she'd have the chance to rise above the smut and come clean. The wheels of justice grind slowly, but they do grind.

I wasn't surprised when her charges were dropped. Even her distracters who hated her were not surprised. The only person who was surprised, oddly, was her criminal lawyer, Murtha.

Although she said she had received "hundreds of press calls," Linda and her lawyer decided not to do much until they figured out how to best move forward. That was strange. Why would Joe Murtha pass up media requests to speak about, as he had called it, "the most notorious—and shameful—political prosecution of this century"?[393]

Who would have something to lose with Linda's public vindication? Could it be Hillary, who was campaigning for the junior New York Senate seat at the time?[394] Who had a lot to lose, like an election, had Linda's trial proceeded and revealed she was right? The Clinton-Lewinsky scandal wasn't about sex or Hillary's vast right-wing conspiracy, but it was about suborning perjury, witness tamping, and obstruction of justice. Now that evidence wouldn't see daylight. Would it help or hurt Hillary's election bid if Bill's salacious, degrading, and dishonest conduct was resurrected? Nah, the timing must be a coincidence. As the Clintons would say; nothing here, move on.

As for Murtha, although his stint as Linda's criminal lawyer was over, he wasn't going anywhere. Days after the criminal case was dismissed, he finagled his way into her civil case against the Clinton Department of Defense for illegally leaking her FBI file (ultimately the case was settled). Then he offered to stay on to handle Linda's media relations. She was thrilled because he was the only person she trusted. *Isn't he a criminal lawyer?*

Now telling her story became her number one priority and Murtha's too. That was astonishing considering no matter how many questions I asked or faxed him or how many phone calls and trips I had taken to meet with Linda, Murtha never explained anything. He never provided me with any documentation that would vindicate his client and expose "the most notorious—and shameful—political prosecution of this century." Even stranger, when I was able to meet with her it seemed like he was shadowing her with his constant check-in phone calls. After Linda spoke with him, her paranoia soared. Instantly she would backtrack and water down something she had told me earlier about the Clintons, and switch to petty, gossipy Monica stories. It was frustrating; one minute she was courageous and brave, ready to make amends and tell the whole truth, then the next moment she would crater, rinse and repeat. Would she stand tall this time or buckle again? I wondered, debating whether or not I should give writing her story—factually—another try.

If she kept true to her word, a mea culpa, and actually blew the whistle, she could do a lot of good. Americans deserved to know what was happening in their White House—that even Linda, the so-called Clinton-Lewinsky whistleblower, could be corrupted and compromised by the Clintons. If she would tell the truth, I would write it. So I gave it one last try and met with her again.

It was wishful thinking.

Chapter 19: Sunlight

"No one can serve two masters, for either he will hate the one and love the other, or he will be devoted to the one and despise the other. You cannot serve God and money."

—Matthew 6:24 (ESV)

"Well, I can tell you this," Linda's lead attorney, Joe Murtha, insisted to me on the phone, "despite all the work and all the money that has been made, I've never made as much money as Linda Tripp has in a year. Let me tell you."

And so he did. It was July 18, 2000. I'd been sparring with him over his latest incarnation in Linda's life since seeing her again. It was bad enough that someone had leaked a story in the press the day before that Linda was "hustling" a book with my agent without my knowledge, but at that moment that was the least of my concerns.[395] Now Murtha was acting as her literary agent with big plans to be a Hollywood movie producer by selling her story (using my work product). It was nuts. Naturally, any questions I asked him about the Clintons and her case he dodged.

Perhaps I was a cynic but I'd had enough of Murtha's non-stop stonewalling while faking a protective and facilitating posture while he controlled Linda and tried to control me.

By then I saw Linda's lawyer as a wolf in sheep's clothing. Whether he was interested in the money or he really was the Clinton plant that Linda worried about when I first met with her, or a combination of both, I'll leave for you to decide.

His fishy role didn't end with his Hollywood dreams. No, Linda's criminal/civil lawyer-media advisor-literary agent-movie producer also offered to be her personal messenger service. Yes, it is true because Linda's fax machine was broken, I was supposed to fax anything I wrote that I wanted her to review to his Baltimore office, then he'd rush it over to Linda's house in Columbia (to be helpful, of course). She refused to accept a couple hundred dollars from me to buy a new fax machine. It was ridiculous. Thank God I'd pushed play and record on *my* Radio Shack tape recorder long ago. Ironically, I was the one who now needed an insurance policy to protect the truth.

Murtha blathered on. "It's true," he continued. "But that's an interesting point because a lot of people have a misperception that in some way I've gotten rich off of this case. And ahh, that's far from the truth. I was merely an associate when this began, and if someone else profited it certainly wasn't me. I mean I'm tired," he bellyached. "I may have bought a farm but let me tell you I earned every friggin penny I made ... Not only did I earn it, we had to go out and raise it ... I mean there's nobody paying us other than the people who were kind enough to send in the donations."

And that's true. Linda was not responsible for her legal bills. Her legal defense fund was funded by hardworking people who sent her whatever they could, believing they were helping her in her "fight for justice" against the Clinton White House. "Linda R. Tripp legal defense fund" was a corporation, donations were not tax deductible. It was structured so that her lawyers would be compensated through donations sent to the legal defense fund. Meanwhile, I'd watched Murtha living large, buying a farm and jetting off to Los Angeles and New York without a courtroom on his itinerary.

And Linda? A test of someone's honesty is the presence or absence of hypocrisy. Now that her criminal jeopardy was gone, before my eyes, she was becoming like the Clintons, and like everything she once despised; dishonest, self-serving, and selectively truthful—she wanted revenge. Incredibly, she was crying victim again, although she had sat back and allowed others to be victimized by the Clintons—who also cried victim.

I knew it would take courage for her to admit her role in towing the Clinton White House line during the investigations and blow the whistle, but if a high profile person is supposedly fighting for justice against the Clinton White House (and soliciting donations in that fight), then they must stand tall and fight with the truth—warts and all.

So when Murtha tried to railroad me with my agent, into a despicably lopsided contract that in part took editorial control over my work product (that I funded), and Linda sat by and demanded that I agree to remain in Virginia until *she* decided I completed writing her story, I had a choice to make; do I join their unholy alliance to make a few bucks that I really needed or walk?

I prayed for guidance and I received it. After seven months of dealing with her off and on, knowing what I knew and could verify, I couldn't co-sign myself to her hell and sacrifice the truth to protect the Clintons and cover up for Linda too because she was "gutless" and had towed the Clinton line. *Thou shalt not bear false witness.* So I walked, taking my work with me and protected myself. Linda was free to write whatever she wanted to write but she and her lawyer were not free to use my work to publish untruths or to dictate my life. I was not going to participate in what would become their Clintonesque publicity stunt disguised as news.

Ten days after my fateful conversation with Linda's lawyer on July 28, 2000, Murtha ludicrously accused me of sabotaging her book in the *Washington Post*.[396]

What followed could have been a bad movie. After the *Post* story ran my phone started ringing. Questions from the outrageous to cryptic poured in. One "journalist" wanted to know how much Linda really ate while another asked if I could prove that Vince Foster was murdered. I received warnings that my apartment could be broken into, plus a suggestion to make copies of what I had and hide it, quick. I did. It was wild.

Next what I feared would happen, happened when Linda broke her silence shortly thereafter. Thank God my hands were clean of it. Instead of ridding herself of malice, deceit, and hypocrisy, by telling the truth and warning America of the corruption and rot that she experienced and succumbed to in the Clinton White House (that we are now witnessing in the Obama administration), Linda wanted glory. She came out swinging and went on the attack.

Together with her lawyer, Murtha, they did what Hillary and Bill Clinton did; they re-wrote history, and played the victim card. Lining up back-to-back "Exclusive: Breaking Her Silence" interviews at Murtha's "urging,"

Linda hit the media circuit and embraced the falsehood that she was a whistleblower.[397]

"I'd Do It All Over Again," blared the first headline in the now defunct *George Magazine* that reported Linda "had absolutely no regrets."[398] That headline launched her all over the news just as the latest Clinton scandal, Pardongate, was making headlines, and Linda with a straight face claimed, "Had there been more Linda Tripps in the Clinton White House, what has happened since, may well have been avoided."[399] Recall, in Pardongate, President Clinton granted clemency to FLAN terrorists from the Puerto Rican separatist group; Weather Underground terrorists (of President Obama's friend, William Ayers' fame); drug dealers; and fugitive, tax evader, financier Marc Rich, who was involved in oil deals with Iran and Iraq to name a few.

The "journalist," who Linda and Murtha granted the world "exclusive" aided in their fundraising scheme when she partook in media interviews to promote her ABC *20/20* exclusive interview. "In fact [Linda Tripp] is a million dollars in debt to her lawyers," the "journalist" said.[400]

During Linda's media blitz, she cried poverty and took potshots: "To those who say I documented Monica for a book, well, where is that book? I've never taken a nickel—nothing. This was the story of the century; no one could get access, so the 'money flying around' was ridiculous," she said. "But I chose not to participate because I am not the story. I turned down millions—even though I drive a nine-year-old car and live in a rented house. It's debilitating to owe hundreds of thousands in legal bill, because unlike Ms. Lewinsky, I am on my own."[401]

Linda also contradicted her grand jury testimony when she said this, for instance: "Following Vince [Foster's] death, I had been interrogated by the OIC and was far more forthcoming about Vince than the Clinton people would have liked. What I said in those confidential depositions trickled back to Bruce Lindsey, the president, Mrs. Clinton. And I was asked to leave." [402]

What confidential depositions? As Linda testified, she was transferred from the White House to the Pentagon after she voiced concerns to presidential aide Bruce Lindsey. "I've been loyal [to the Clinton administration]. I have worked through these horrible investigations ... My feeling was that for some reason I was not thought to be on the team ... and I had not at that point done anything not to be on the team."[403] By her own admission,

Linda towed the Clinton line. She did not blow the whistle in 1994 or 1998, unless she now wants to dispute her sworn testimony.

A few short months later, Linda intensified her victim posture when she remerged in the press and claimed she was "unknowingly fired" from her non-Pentagon job, after she "refused to resign" regardless of the fact that *every* political appointee resigns when a new administration comes in. She knew that, we discussed it, just like every other political appointee knows that. It was pitiful.[404]

It gets worse; her icy slope became a fall. Eight months later Linda played politics when she doubled her fundraising pleas when this story made news: "Linda Tripp is crying poverty in a fund-raising letter sent to Republican supporters … she says she can no longer pay her rent, buy food, or support her family … she's sinking under a mountain of debt including more than $2 million in legal bills."[405] (Linda's civil suit with the Department of Defense was settled for $595,000, not $2 million. All the materials produced during the discovery phase remain confidential.)[406] In addition to begging for money, she circulated a petition for people to sign demanding that newly elected President George W. Bush give her a job.

It didn't have to be that way. The road she chose reminded me of the story when the Lord told Moses and Aaron to speak to the rock to bring forth water to his thirsty people and livestock found in Numbers 20:12 (AMP). Instead of obeying the Lord as was commanded, Moses was arrogant when he said, "Hear now, you rebels; must we bring you water out of this rock?" and he struck the rock with a rod—twice.

"God held Moses responsible for not obeying Him exactly. Obedience to His will is vitally important, whether we understand His purpose or not. The motto 'God's will: nothing more; nothing less; nothing else; at any cost' would have been priceless to Moses and Aaron that day, if they had only followed it." [407]

It would have been priceless to Linda too, had she returned to her Christian faith that she had strayed from while serving under the Clintons, and shown contrition, sought redemption, by telling the truth—and actually blown the whistle. She should have spoken and not boldly struck out. What a price she paid.

Lies beget lies. Linda's transgressions have a deeper meaning than may first appear obvious. For all of her efforts, excuses, and justifications to protect the Clintons, to keep her job, ultimately she lost it. What could have been a victory for Linda, and a victory for honest government and account-ability, also could have been the demise of the special justice and rights class system for the ruling elite that has taken a grip on America.

Linda's Clinton White House experience demonstrates a larger and sad-der truth about morality. It speaks to how men sell their souls in install-ments, succumbing to each crisis of conscience. Then one day they wake up unrecognizable to their former selves. Don't think it can't happen to you. Stand now. Stand always.

And the thanks Linda's received for her loyalty by playing on Team Clin-ton at the expense of the truth? Here's the kicker: the Clinton White House knew from the start that *Linda never wanted to write a book, she never conspired with Hillary's vast right-wing conspiracy to bring down President Clinton,* but the Clintons with the help of the media and their surrogates, smeared, vili-fied, and destroyed her anyways—now that's evil. As Saul Alinsky teaches: *the ends justify the means.*

According to a dirt-digging memo written by one of the Clintons' pri-vate investigators addressed to the Clintons' former Deputy Chief of Staff Harold Ickes, Hillary's hammer (who spearheaded her 2008 failed presi-dential bid): *"Linda Tripp may herself have only been used ..."*[408] The memo was dated one day before Hillary's infamous *Today Show* appearance where she falsely blamed the phony vast right-wing conspiracy with Linda in the starring role. This is Hillary's secret police in action. The prying, snooping, intrusive memo unearths dirt on Monica Lewinsky and Monica's mother as well.

Ickes testified during the Clinton-Lewinsky investigation that he was in contact with President Clinton and Hillary when the story broke "... it would have included myself ... [and Hollywood image maker] Mr. Thoma-son," he said.[409] One would have to suspend disbelief to think that Ickes neglected to tell Hillary and Bill what he uncovered. *"Linda Tripp may herself have only been used ..."* Now you know how corrupt government offi-cials stay in power, how they will do and say anything to keep that power, and the strategies and tactics they use to do so. You are disposable just like Linda was.

The solution: Put your trust in God, not in false idols. Turn away from the false salvation that never comes from Saul Alinsky's man-made pro-gressive social justice philosophy. Break the right/left paradigm that ben-efits politicians and return to what is right and wrong. If confronted with corruption, get proof to expose it, stop it—if you don't you will become part of it. Demand that Executive Order 1273 mandating that all federal employees "shall disclose waste, fraud, abuse and corruption to appropriate authorities" be enforced—no matter which political party is in power.[410] If corruption within government is not held accountable now and past injustices righted, the Obama administration's (with Hillary's State Department) scandals, like the "Fast and Furious" gunrunner operation, Solyndra, and WikiLeaks, will be swept aside to join the Clinton investigations into the re-written dust bin of history.

It's up to you, the individual, to restore America to her exceptional glory, as one Nation under God, indivisible, with liberty and justice for all. Linda's experience should serve as cautionary tale; how one person can be a force for good or for evil. It's your choice.

We end now as we began, "Take no part in the unfruitful works of darkness, but instead expose them."—Ephesians 5:11 ESV

A note to my secular, atheist, agnostic and humanist friends and readers

We are all free to believe or to *not believe* in God. With or without the bible verses, *The Whistleblower* is the same story. If you have a problem with references to God and to Christianity skip over the scriptures that open each chapter and a couple paragraphs towards the end of the last chapter. When reporting on an ideology dedicated to Lucifer, I believe it is prudent to counter Lucifer with God.

That said, I think it is fair to say we are all flawed. I also believe that a liar and a hypocrite, be it a person "of faith" or a "non-believer," is still a liar and a hypocrite just like corruption, whether it appears on the Right or the Left of the political spectrum is still corruption.

A note on sourcing and documentation

The quotes in this book are real unless otherwise cited as a reconstruction. They come from my personal notes, research, and tapes. Occasionally they are from secondary printed media sources that are sourced in the endnotes. Although Linda and I discussed everything that has been covered in this book, often I quote from Linda's testimony and public statements to ensure accuracy.

Please visit marinkapeschmann.com/endnotes for additional endnote sourcing, links, videos, documentation, acknowledgements, resources, and contact information.

A comprehensive, though not an exhaustive bibliography

Several books have been written about the Clinton era. They have all proved invaluable, most notably: Bill and Hillary Clinton's autobiographies, *My Life* and *Living History; Uncovering Clinton* by Michael Isikoff; *The Hunting of the President*, by Joe Conason and Gene Lyons; *Blinded by the Right* by David Brock; *High Crimes and Misdemeanors* by Ann Coulter; *All Too Human—a political education*, by George Stephanopoulos; *Because He Could*, by Dick Morris and Eileen McGann; *Sell Out*, by David Schippers; *The First Partner, Hillary Rodham Clinton*, by Joyce Milton; *My FBI*, by Louis J. Freeh; *A Vast*

Right Wing Conspiracy, by Jeffrey Toobin; *American Rhapsody,* by Joe Esterzhas; *For Love of Politics: Bill and Hillary Clinton: The White House Years*, by Sally Bedell Smith; *Monica's Story*, by Andrew Morton; *Unlimited Access*, by Gary Aldrich; *The Strange Death of Vincent Foster*, by Christopher Ruddy; *Rules for Radicals,* by Saul D. Alinsky; The Office of Independent Counsel's investigations; White House press briefings; *9/11 Commission Report*; *Holy War Inc*, by Peter L. Bergen; *Losing Bin Laden*, by Rich Miniter; Laurence Wright's *The Looming Tower*; and the *9/11 Commission Report*.

Endnotes

1   Saul Alinsky, *Rules for Radicals,* (Vintage, October 23, 1989).

2   Peter Slevin, "For Clinton and Obama, a Common Ideological Touchstone," *Washington Post*, March 25, 2007.

3   Camille Paglia, "Hillary Clinton's candidacy has done feminism no favour," *The Telegraph,* May 24, 2008.

4   Hillary Clinton, *Living History,* (Simon & Schuster, June 9 2003).
    Also see: Bill Clinton, *My Life,* (Alfred A. Knopf, 2004).

5   Jennifer Epstein, "Newt Gingrich: Obama is Clinton's 3rd term," *Politico,* January 21, 2011.

6   Carol E. Lee, "Obama exits, Clinton keeps talking," *Politico,* December 10, 2010.

7   Chris Matthews, "President of the World: The Bill Clinton Phenomenon," *MSNBC*, updated February 11, 2011. "There isn't a single political figure today with the global reach and influence of Bill Clinton—a former U.S. president turned humanitarian and diplomat extraordinaire. This Presidents' Day, *MSNBC's* Chris Matthews will take viewers behind the scenes of Clinton's life in the one-hour documentary "President of the World: The Bill Clinton Phenomenon."

8   Dispatches, *BBC News,* January 6, 1998.

9   Matt Drudge, "Newsweek Kills Story on White House Intern. Blockbuster Report: 23-Year Old, Former White House Intern, Sex Relationship with President," *Drudge Report*, January 17, 1998.

10 Matt Drudge, "Controversy Swirls Around Tapes of Former White House Intern, as Starr Moves In!!" *Drudge Report*, January 20, 1998.

11 "Clinton Accused. Key Player: Paula Jones," *Washington Post,* October 2, 1998.

12 "Referral to the United States House of Representatives pursuant to Title 28, United States Code 595(c), Submitted by the Office of the Independent Counsel," *Starr Report,* September 9, 1998.

13 Betty Currie deposition, *Starr Report*, January 27, 1998, p. 560, see p. 78.

14 Hillary Clinton, *Living History*, (First Scribner Trade paperback edition, 2004), p. 440.

15 Susan Schmidt, Peter Baker and Toni Locy, "Clinton Accused of Urging Aide to Lie," *Washington Post,* January 21, 1998; p. A1.

16   Susan Schmidt, Peter Baker and Toni Locy, "Clinton Accused of Urging Aide to Lie," *Washington Post,* January 21, 1998; p. A1.

17   Dick Morris, "The Clinton Years," *ABC News Nightline/ PBS Frontline*, January 16, 2001.

18   Bill Clinton, *The Oprah Winfrey Show,* June 22, 2004.

19   President Clinton with Jim Lehrer, *PBS News Hour Interview*, January 21, 1998.

20   R.W. Apple Jr., "The President Under Fire: The Power Broker; Jordan Trades Stories with Clinton, and Offers Counsel," *New York Times*, January 25, 1998.

21   "A Chronology: Key Moments in the Clinton-Lewinsky Saga," *CNN.*

22   List of deceased persons reportedly associated with the Clinton Administration, (left on Linda Tripp's chair by Monica Lewinsky, according to Tripp), Judicial Watch.

23   "Tripp's Life Threatened, attorney says," *The Atlanta Journal and Constitution*, May 27, 1998; p. 12a. "Asked whether Tripp was taken to a safe house after the allegations surfaced, Zaccagnini said, "Linda Tripp … was the subject of a lot of press scrutiny and there were some threats made against her life. As a result, the FBI, in conjunction with Starr's office, decided to move her to a secure location."

24   "Mrs. Tripp says she is thinking about doing a book," *Associated Press*, February 16, 1999.

25   "From Threat to Threat," *9/11 Commission Report,* (Barnes & Nobles Publishing, Inc., 2004), p. 177.

26   "ABC New Polls Tripp with Bin Laden, Hussein," via *Drudge Report* 1998..

27   Joe Conason & Gene Lyons, *The Hunting of the President: The Ten-Year Campaign to Destroy Bill and Hillary Clinton,* (St. Martin's Press, 2000).

28   Dan Froomkin, "Case Closed," *Washington Post*, updated December 3, 1998.

29   *Paula Jones Complaint Against President Clinton & Danny Ferguson,* filed May 6, 1994, via Lectric Law Library.

30   Margaret Calson, "With Friends Like These …" *Time Magazine.* Feb. 9, 1998. Also see: Josh Chafetz, "The Immutable Laws of Maureen Dowd," *Weekly Standard,* October 14, 2002.

31   Jonah Goldberg, "Hard Tripp," *National Review,* November 23, 1998.

32   Linda Tripp Indictment, *Hannity and Colmes, Fox News*, August 3, 1999, via High-Beam Research.

33   Geraldo Rivera, MSNBC's *Rivera Live*, June 26, 1998.

34   Tom Brokaw interviews Bob Woodward, "The story behind 'Deep Throat,'" *Dateline, NBC,* July 6, 2005.

35   "Clinton Accused. Key Player: Paula Jones," *Washington Post,* October 2, 1998.

36   Susan Schmidt, "Starr Brings Third Indictment Against Hubbell," *Washington Post,* November 14, 1998; p. A1.

37   "Why we ran the Henry Hyde story," *Salon.com,* September 16, 1998.

38   Jonathan D. Salant, "Hillary Clinton Fundraisers Indicted for Reimbursing Campaign Contributions," *Bloomberg*, February 17, 2011.

39   Patricia Towle, "Linda Tripp Plastic Surgery Miracle," *National Enquirer*, December 1999, p. 9.

40   David Johnston, "Jurors in Maryland Indict Linda Tripp in Lewinsky Tapes," *New York Times,* July 31, 1999.

41 LindaTripp.com see marinkapeschmann.com/endnotes

42 "Obama: I will be the Democratic nominee," *CNN Politics,* June 3, 2008.

43 Jack Cafferty, "Should Hillary Clinton challenge Obama in 2012?" *CNN,* January 28, 2010.

44 Dick Morris on New Clinton Books, *Hannity & Colmes, Fox News,* June 4, 2007.

45 Joshua Green, "The Front-Runner's Fall," *The Atlantic.com,* September 2008.

46 Rick Lyman, "The Rise, the Fall, and Now a New Day," *New York Times.* July 8, 2003. Author's note: After prison McNall published, *Fun While It Lasted: My Rise and Fall in the Land of Fame and Fortune,* (Hyperion, 2003).

47 "Democrats Pushed for Tripp Wiretap Probe, Lawyers Say," *Associated Press,* July 10, 1998.

48 Saul Alinsky, *Rules for Radicals,* (Vintage, October 23, 1989), p. 117.

49 Peter Slevin, "For Clinton and Obama, a Common Ideological Touchstone," *Washington Post*, March 25, 2007.

50 Saul Alinsky, *Rules for Radicals,* (Vintage, October 23, 1989), p. 128.

51 "Obama on small-town Pa.: Clinging to religion, guns, xenophobia," *Politico,* April 11, 2008.

52 Department of Homeland Security: Rightwing Extremism: Current Economic and Political Climate Fueling Resurgence in Radicalization and Recruitment. 2009.

53 Saul Alinsky, *Rules for Radicals,* (Vintage, October 23, 1989), p. 144.

54 Jonathan Allen and John Bresnahan, "Sources, Joe Biden likened tea parties to terrorists," *Politico,* August 2, 2011.

55 Saul Alinsky, *Rules for Radicals,* (Vintage, October 23, 1989), p. 10.

56 Patricia Towle, "Linda Tripp Plastic Surgery Miracle," *National Enquirer,* December 1999, p. 9.

57 Dr. Geoffrey Keyes discusses Linda Tripp's Plastic Surgery with Charles Gibson, *ABC News, Good Morning America*, January 24, 2000. Also see: Barbara Walters and Cynthia McFadden, "More Than Skin Deep Criticism Compels Women to Have Plastic Surgery," *ABC News 20/20,* January 28, 2000. Also see: Dr. Keyes and Jack Klugman, *Fox News Live, Fox News,* February 24, 2000. Also see: Anne-Marie O'Neill, John Hannah, Alexandra Hardy, Joanna Blonska, and Elizabeth McNeil, "Change of Face," *People Magazine,* January 17, 2000, p. 124-126. David Letterman, CBS *David Letterman Show.*

58 "Al Qaeda Associated Charged in Attack on USS Cole Attempted Attack on Another U.S. Naval Vessel," *Department of Justice Press Release,* May 15, 2003.

59 "Oct. 12, 2000: USS Cole Attacked in Yemen," *ABC, World News.*

60 Katharine Q. Seelye, "Barack Obama, asked about drug history, admits he inhaled," *New York Times,* October 24, 2006.
    Also see: "Putting on Ayers," *Snopes.com.* Last update: December 6, 2008.
    Also see: Rick Moran, "It's Getting Crowded Under Obama's Bus," *American Thinker*, June 12, 2008. Also see: Peter Wallsten, "Allies of Palestinians see a friend in Obama, *Los Angeles Times,* April 10, 2008.

61 Federal Bureau of Investigations, See background checks.

62 "Use of crack, hallucinogens hung up White House staff," *Associated Press,* July 18, 1996.

Also see: Mary Gordon, "Clinton Administration overruled the Secret Service," *Associated Press,* July 17, 1996.

63   "Rose Zamaria, a Key Player in the President's 'Inner Circle,'" *Los Angeles Times*, October 20, 1992.

64   John Podhoretz, "Beaten and Bushed – Sam Skinner's ineffective management of White House during George Bush year," *Washington Monthly,* October 1993.

65   "It All Began in a Place Called Hope, President Bill Clinton," *White House biography of the President.*

66   Michael Crowley, "Is this goodbye? *The Guardian,* June 1, 2008. "In many ways, Barack Obama's campaign has eerily echoed Bill Clinton's 1992 candidacy. Bill, too, campaigned on the themes of change and hope. (He was even 'the Man from Hope.') Clinton promised to cure a national malaise (in 1992 a recession was under way – prompting the famous Clinton slogan, 'It's the economy, stupid'). And like Obama, Bill contrasted his youth and freshness against an entrenched Washington insider: George H.W. Bush, father of the current president. Clinton was elected by a comfortable margin. On his inauguration day, he was just 46 years old – a year younger than Obama is today." Also see: "The hope-and-change index," *The Economist,* January 19, 2009. Also see: "Obama: I will be the Democratic nominee," *CNN,* June 3, 2008.

67   Saul Alinsky, *Rules for Radicals,* (Vintage, October 23, 1989), p. 12.

68   Chris Bury: "An Interview with James Carville, The Clinton Years," Interview, *PBS Frontline & ABC's Nightline,* June 2000.

69   "Clinton's Debate Moment," 1992 Presidential Debate, *CSPAN.*

70   George Stephanopoulos, *All Too Human,* (Little Brown and Company, 1999).

71   "Bill Clinton's Draft Letter," *PBS Frontline,* Interview hosted by Ted Koppel with then Governor Clinton follows, *ABC Nightline* Transcript. February 1992.
      Also see: "Bill Clinton and Gennifer Flowers – 1999." *Washington Post,* (Larry J. Sabato) 1998.

72   "Obama says he didn't know his aunt's illegal status," *Associated Press,* November 1, 2008.

73   "Clinton Wins Decisive Margin In Voter Poll Across Nation After 12 Years of G.O.P. Rule," *New York Times*, November 4, 1992, p. A 1.

74   Andrew H. Card, *The Office of Presidential Transition,* November 18, 1992.

75   Michael Bardaro, "For Bloomberg, A Round to Remember," *New York Times,* September 19, 2010. Also see: Vernon Jordan interview with Katie Courie, The Inauguration of Barack Obama, *CBS News.* January 2009. Also see: R.W. Apple Jr., "The President Under Fire: The Power Broker; Jordan Trade Stories with Clinton and Offers Counsel," *New York Times,* January 25, 1998.

76   Joe Eszterhas, *American Rhapsody,* (Alfred A. Knopf, July 2000). IBID

77   Joe Eszterhas, *American Rhapsody,* (Alfred A. Knopf, July 2000), p. 117.

78   "Defense Department settles with Linda Tripp," *Associated Press,* January 3, 2003.

79   Eamon Javers, "Robert Rubin returns," *Politico,* April 8, 2011.

80   "Clinton touts commander-in-chief credentials," *CNN,* April 25, 2008.

81   Linda Tripp, *Larry King Live, CNN,* February 16, 1999.

82   Sally Bedell Smith, "Why Hillary Clinton let husband Bill seduce any woman in sight," *Extracted from The Love of Politics: Bill and Hillary Clinton: The White House Years,* 2008.

83 Sally Bedell Smith, "Why Hillary Clinton let husband Bill seduce any woman in sight," *Extracted from The Love of Politics: Bill and Hillary Clinton: The White House Years,* 2008.

84 "Governor Bill Clinton's Interview with Steve Kroft," Transcript: *CBS's 60 Minutes,* January 26, 1992.

85 Eric Pooley, "Kiss But Don't Tell," *Time Magazine,* June 24, 2001.

86 Dan Glaister, "The Pellicano Files," *The Guardian,* April 19, 2006.

87 John Podesta, Bio, Center for American Progress. Also see: Ben Smith, "John Podesta to step down as Center for American Progress president," *Politico,* October 24, 2011.

88 David Paul Kuhn, "Vacation Politics, "Kerry Hits the Slopes; Bush Prefers His Texas Ranch,'" *CBS News,* March 18, 2004. Also see: Byron York, "The Facts About Clinton and Terrorism," *National Review,* September 11, 2006.

89 Ann Devroy, "Clinton Fires White House Worker Bees," *Washington Post,* February 7, 1993, p. A 19. "White House communications director George Stephanopoulos said the president, in trying to reduce the size and cost of the White House staff, could not exempt anyone, even longtime career workers. He said [Clinton] "is committed" to reducing the staff not just on paper but in reality. Asked why Clinton chose the lower-paid, unprotected career workers for his first layoffs, Stephanopoulos said everyone who works in the White House would be affected by the belt-tightening."

90 Donald Devine, "Why President Clinton's Reinvention of Government is Not Working," *Heritage, Foundation,* December 28, 1993.

91 Robert W. Ray, Independent Counsel, *Final Report of the Independent Counsel* (In Re: Madison Guaranty Savings & Loan Associations) of Matters Related to the White House Travel office.
See: A: Watkins Statements Regarding Mrs. Clinton's Involvement in the Travel office firings. Watkins, GJ 2/28/95 at 51-53. Also see Watkins Int. 6/13/00 at 3 (describing Mrs. Clinton's discussion—as communicated to Watkins—with former Lady Rosalyn Carter about "getting their own people on board"). p. 23

92 Hillary denies using profanity and cursing, however, Linda is not the only person who has heard it. See: (i) "Where is the G-damn f–king flag? I want the G-damn f–king flag up every f–king morning at f–king sunrise."
Ronald Kessler, *Inside The White House,* p. 244 – Hillary to the staff at the Arkansas Governor's mansion on Labor Day, 1991) (ii)"You sold out, you mother f–ker! You sold out!"
Joseph Califano, *Inside: A Public and Private Life,* (PublicAffairs, Perseus Books Group, 2004), p. 213 – Hillary yelling at Democrat lawyer. (iii)"F–k off! It's enough that I have to see you s–t-kickers every day, I'm not going to talk to you too!! Just do your G-d d—n job and keep your mouth shut."
Christopher Anderson, *American Evita: Clinton's Path to Power,* (Harper Collins, 2004,) p. 90 – Hillary to her State Trooper bodyguards after one of them greeted her with "Good morning."(iv)"If you want to remain on this detail, get your f–king a– over here and grab those bags!"
Joyce Milton, *The First Partner: Hillary Rodham Clinton,* (William Morrow, 1999), p. 259 – Hillary to a Secret Service Agent who was reluctant to carry her luggage because he wanted to keep his hands free in case of an incident.)

(v)"Get f–ked! Get the f–k out of my way!!! Get out of my face!!!"
Carl Limbacher, *Hillary's Scheme: Inside the Next Clinton's Ruthless Agenda to Take the White House,* "p. 89 – Hillary's various comments to her Secret Service detail agents.)
(vi) "Stay the f–k back, stay the f–k away from me! Don't come within ten yards of me, or else! Just f–king do as I say, Okay!!!?" Gary Aldrich, *Unlimited Access: A FBI Agent Inside the Clinton White House,* (Regnery Publishing), p.139 – Hillary screaming at her Secret Service detail.)

93   Michael Waldaman, Chief White House speech writer from 1995-1999, "The Clinton Years," *PBS Frontline & ABC Nightline* Interview with Chris Bury, September 2000.

94   Sally Bedell Smith, "Why Hillary Clinton let husband Bill seduce any woman in sight," *Extracted from For the Love of Politics: Bill and Hillary Clinton: The White House Years,* 2008.

95   "President Bill Clinton's Address before a Joint Session of Congress on the State of the Union," February 17, 1993.

96   Stephen Dian, "Memo outlines backdoor 'amnesty' plan," *Washington Times,* July 29, 2010.
Also see: Stephen Dinan, "House chairman, Obama uncle's got 'backdoor amnesty,'" *Washington Times,* September 9, 2011.

97   Chris Bury, "Interview with David Gergen, The Clinton Years," *ABC Nightline/PBS Frontline,* June 2000.

98   "1993: World Trade Center bomb terrorizes New York," *BBC News,* February 26, 1993.

99   *Linda Tripp, Larry King Live, CNN,* February 16, 1999.

100   Linda Tripp, *Larry King Live*, CNN, February 16, 1999.

101   Bernie Nussbaum, Mark Curriden, *ABA Journal,* March 2, 2009.

102   Ruth Marcus (Mike Isikoff staff writer contributed), "Clinton Nominates Reno at Justice," *Washington Post*, February 12, 1993, p.A01. "In December, Clinton nominated corporate lawyer Zoe E. Baird, who was forced to withdraw because she had violated immigration and tax laws in hiring illegal immigrants. He was poised to name federal judge Kimba M. Wood before she withdrew last week after the disclosure that she had also employed an illegal immigrant to care for her child." Also see: "Nominees, problems with hired help," *Associated Press,* January 9, 2001.

103   Scott Whitlock, "Media Ignore Politicized Clinton Justice Department," *Media Research Center.* "ABC Frets Over Dismissal of 8 U.S. Attorneys; Ignored Clinton's Firing of 93 Attorneys," *NewsBusters,* March 13, 2007. "According to a *Washington Post* article by Dan Balz that ran on March 26 of that year, there was nothing unusual about the dismissals: Presidential spokesman George Stephanopoulos said it was not unusual for a president to ask for such resignations, although Republicans said presidents in the past have not asked for mass resignations, replacing them over a period of time as replacements were found. Stephanopoulos said only those U.S. attorneys who are in the middle of trials will be allowed to continue working and said an interim appointee could capably pick up [U.S. attorney for the District of Columbia Jay B.] Stephens's investigation of the House Post Office scandal, with no serious disruption or political interference."

104 Robert W. Ray, Independent Counsel, *Final Report of the Independent Counsel In Re: Madison Guaranty Savings & Loan Association,* January 5, 2001 See: The Clintons, the McDougals, and the Whitewater Development Company. p. 1.

105 Michael Haddigan, "Susan McDougal Gets 2 Years for Fraud Tied to Whitewater," *Washington Post*, August 21, 1996, p. A14.

106 Brian Ross and Rhonda Schwartz, "The Rezko Connection: Obama's Achilles Heel?" *ABC News*, January 10, 2008.

107 Obama Political Fundraiser Tony Rezko Found Guilty on 16 Counts in Corruption Trial," *Associated Press,* June 5, 2008.

108 George Stephanpoulos, *All Too Human*, (Little Brown and Company, 1999), p. 231-232.

109 Whitewater Special Report, Timeline, *Washington Post,* September 1993.

110 Essay; Vincent Foster's "Can of Worms." William Safire, *New York Times,* July 24, 1995.

111 Karen Ball, "Notes Show Foster Feared Whitewater," *Daily News,* July 15, 1995. Also see: *The Washington Times* article July 15, 1995.

112 Joseph Murtha bio, Irwin Green & Dexter, LLP. Note: Currently Murtha works at the law firm Miller Murtha & Psoras L.L.C.

113 Jake Sherman and John Bresnahan, "Liberals launch anti-Darrell Issa crusade," *Politico*, February 15, 2011.

114 Robert L. Jackson, "Former White House Travel Chief Faces Theft Charges: Probe: Billy R. Dale is accused of embezzling more than $68,000. Associates say he is the victim of a witch hunt." *Los Angeles Times*, December 8, 1994.

115 Lawyer Sees Travel Office Indictment, David Johnston, *New York Times,* December 5, 1994.

116 Hillary Clinton, *Living History,* (First Scribner Trade paperback edition, 2004), p. 172.

117 *Former Director of White House Travel Office Indicted*, Press Release, Wednesday, December 7, 1994.

118 Saul Alinsky, *Rules for Radicals*, (Vintage, October 23, 1989), p. 26.

119 Toni Lacy, "For White House Travel Office, A Two-Year Trip of Trouble," *Washington Post*, February 27, 1995; p. A04.

120 Harry Thomason, More on the White House Travel Snafu, *Larry King Live, CNN,* May 25, 1993. Mr. Thomason: "This was somebody in the travel office. And so he called me, disturbed, and he called the other companies and said, 'I don't guess it's possible to do business with the White House. There seems to be no way for any outside companies to bid.' And so what I did, I basically became a whistle-blower. I told the White House about what I thought was an outrageous practice going on where an office in the U.S. government would not talk to people, talk to businesses about doing business with them – and not that they would do business with them, I mean just to talk to them and consider them. And I found that rather outrageous. So I thought I was being a good citizen, and I told people at the White House."

121 Michael McMenamin, James Oliphant, "All the president's fault—US First Lady Hillary's Clinton's dismissal of public employees," *Reason*, April 1996.

122   Toni Locy, "For White House Travel office, a Two-Year Trip of Trouble," *Washington Post*, February 27, 1995, p. A04.

123   Clinton Chief of Staff Mack McLarty praises Barack Obama, Arkansas rally, October 25, 2008.

124   Hillary Clinton, *Living History*, (First Scribner Trade paperback edition, 2004), p. 173.

125   *Travel office Summary: Jurisdictional Grant to the Independent Counsel: Inclusive*, See: p. 4-5: Thursday, May 13, 1993. 99
a. Jeff Eller and Harry Thomason Advocated Firing the Travel Office Staff Due to Public Relations Concerns. 100
b. After the FBI Understood From Kennedy that the "Highest Levels" within the White House were Involved, The FBI Began an Investigation. 104
i. Kennedy Met With the FBI on the Morning of May 13. 106
ii. During the Afternoon of May 13, Kennedy and Foster Met With the FBI Who Interviewed Cornelius. 108
iii. Foster Decided to Proceed With an Audit Before the FBI Criminal Investigation, for Which the FBI Found "Predication." 110
c. McLarty and Foster Discussed the Travel Office With the First Lady and Discussed the First Lady's Concerns With Other Senior Staff. 113
i. Chief of Staff McLarty Briefed Mrs. Clinton. 113
ii. Vince Foster Met Twice With Mrs. Clinton. 117
iii. McLarty, Watkins, Thomasson, and Foster Discussed Mrs. Clinton's Concerns. 119
d. Watkins Retained Auditors and His Staff Prepared For the Travel Office Review. 123
e. Summary of Allegations Made Relating to the Conduct of the Travel Office. 125
4. Friday, May 14, 1993. 130
a. Peat Marwick Began its Travel Office Review. 130
b. Eller Demanded a Meeting With McLarty. 135
c. Mrs. Clinton and David Watkins Had Their Single Substantiated Pre-Firing Conversation Which Occurred by Telephone. 135
i. Watkins's Description of His Phone Conversation With Mrs. Clinton. 137
a) Watkins's Description of His Conversation With Samuel L. Bowman. 137
b) Watkins's Handwritten Notes of May 31, 1993. 138
c) Watkins's Handwritten Notes of June 2, 1993. 138
d) FBI Interview of Watkins on August 8, 1993. 138
e) Statements Related to or Contained in the Watkins Memorandum. 139
PDF: 255.g.akamaitech.net/7/255/2422/13may20041504/icreport.access.gpo.gov/watkins/toc.pdf

126   Harry Thomason, "More on the White House Travel Snafu," *Larry King Live*, May 25, 1993. See above.

127   David Johnston, "Memo Places Hillary Clinton At Core of Travel Office Case," *New York Times*, January 5, 1996.

128   "McLarty Says He Felt 'Pressure' From First Lady on Travel Office,'" *Los Angeles Times*, August 6, 1996.

129 Michael McMenamin, James Oliphant. "All the president's fault—US First Lady Hillary's Clinton's dismissal of public employees," *Reason*, April 1996.

130 Dee Dee Myers, *White House Press Briefing*, May 20, 1993."Ms. Myers: The FBI interviewed the accountants over the weekend, and so they have some preliminary knowledge. Based on that, the decision was made that it was prudent to go forward with an investigation. Peat Marwick did a review of the finances of the travel office. There's a draft report based on that review, which is now being looked at by the White House counsel. As soon as that has been reviewed and is final, it will be forwarded to the FBI and they will begin an investigation. Q: We were told yesterday that it was not certain that the FBI would investigate, but it was reported this morning that they were investigating..."

131 Toni Locy, "For White House Travel office, a Two-Year Trip of Trouble," *Washington Post*, February 27, 1995, p. A04.

132 George Stephanopoulos, *All Too Human*, (Little Brown and Company, 1999), p. 64.

133 Peter Slevin, "For Clinton and Obama, a Common Ideological Touchstone," *Washington Post*, March 25, 2007.
Also see, Saul Alinsky, *Rules for Radicals*, (Vintage, October 23, 1989), p. 58.

134 "Clinton campaign kills negative story," Ben Smith, *Politico*, September 24, 2007.

135 Phil Bronstein, "Update: Obama Administration punishes reporter for using multimedia, then claims they didn't," *San Francisco Chronicle*, April 28, 2011.

136 Hillary Chabot, "White House shuts out Herald scribe," *Boston Herald*, May 18, 2011. Also see: Salena Zito. "Dangerous Precedent for Press," *Pittsburgh Tribune-Review*, May 30, 2011. Also see: "ABC Reporter: White House Official "Screamed' & 'Cussed' at me for coverage of "Fast and Furious," *The Blaze*, October 4, 2011.

137 President Bill Clinton [at news conference earlier today], More on the White House Travel Snafu, *Larry King Live, CNN*, May 25, 1993.

138 Robert W. Ray, Independent Counsel, *Final Report of the Independent Counsel* (In Re: Madison Guaranty Savings & Loan Associations) of Matters Related to the White House Travel office, See: B. Mrs. Clinton's Regarding her Involvement in the Travel Office Firings.
See: GJ 95-2 Exh. 8 at 5, 7-13. This answer was prefaced by a two-page explanation of how busy Mrs. Clinton was during the relevant period and the fact that her father passed away in early April 1993.

139 Saul Alinsky, *Rules for Radicals*, (Vintage, October 23, 1989), p. 36.

140 David Johnston, "Memo Places Hillary Clinton At Core of Travel Office Case," *New York Times*, January 5, 1996.

141 Robert W. Ray, Independent Counsel, *Final Report of the Independent Counsel* (In Re: Madison Guaranty Savings & Loan Associations) of Matters Related to the White House Travel office, See Conclusion.

142 "Travel Office Legal Fees Total $500,000," *Los Angeles Times*, February 16, 1997. "The Treasury "Department has paid about $500,000 in legal fees for seven former White House travel office employees who were fired four years ago. The biggest chunk of the money, $410,607, went to attorneys for Billy R. Dale, the former travel office director who was acquitted of embezzlement charges. Dale was the only travel office employee who faced legal charges; five of the workers were later rehired

in other government jobs. 'We hope this concludes the long ordeal that the federal government chose to put Billy Dale through,' his attorney, Steven Tabackman said."

143 *The Washington Times,* October 19, 2000.

144 Author's note: Hillary Clinton used the same phrase Linda cited her White House attorney used. See: "Starr's fishing expedition." See, Hillary Clinton, *Living History,* (First Scribner Trade paperback edition, 2004), p. 349.

145 President Bill Clinton, *Starr Report:* June 1998, p. 531 & p. 532.

146 George Stephanpoulos, *All Too Human,* (Little Brown and Company, 1999), p. 250.

147 Robert W. Ray, Independent Counsel, *Final Report of the Independent Counsel* (In Re: Madison Guaranty Savings & Loan Associations) of Matters Related to the White House Travel office, See C: Lack of Cooperation by Witnesses, p. 12. "Witnesses' lack of cooperation took several forms. ...The White House Counsel's Office asserted that an attorney-client privilege existed ... White House...[ordered] private attorneys to instruct their White House staff clients not to answer questions based on the White House's claim of attorney-client privilege ... White House officials failed to search for and provide relevant documents ... in response to Grand Jury subpoenas ... witnesses' responses and document productions were coordinated by the White House Counsel's Office and the witnesses' private attorneys."

148 Peter Baker and Susan Schmidt, "Lewinsky Gets Immunity for Her Testimony," *Washington Post,* July 29, 1998. p. A01. "A White House official said Kendall is seeking to put off Clinton's testimony to force Starr to delay any report on potentially impeachable offenses until after the fall elections and a new Congress convenes in January, and so Clinton will get a chance to learn what Lewinsky says in her testimony. Lawyers for many of the witnesses in Starr's six-month grand jury investigation have participated in a White House joint defense agreement under which they share information. While Lewinsky is not part of the joint defense agreement, information at times has flowed easily in back channels from her lawyers to the Clinton team."

149 Linda Tripp, *Starr Report, Starr Referral, Supplemental Materials, Part III, September 28, 1998,* See July 28, 1998 p. 60.

150 Paul W. Valentine, "Maryland Jury to Probe Tripp's taping," *Washington Post,* July 8, 1998, p. A14.

151 Linda Tripp, *Starr Referral, Supplemental Materials, Part III,* Starr Report, September 28, 1998, p. 4237-4237, See July 16, 98, p. 20-21.

152 "Clinton Rejects Idea of Paying Legal Fees of Fired Travel Office Staff," *Los Angeles Times,* August 2, 1996.

153 Linda Tripp, *Starr Report,* Part III, p. 4277, July 28, 1998, p. 49.

154 *The Columbia Encyclopedia,* Sixth Edition, 2001.

155 *9/11 Commission Report,* (Barnes and Nobles, 2004). Chapter 2; p.72.

156 George Stephanopoulos, *All Too Human,* (Little Brown and Company, 1999), p. 187.

157 Linda Tripp, *Starr Report, Part III,* p. 4276. See July 28, 1998, p. 47.

158 Bill Clinton, *My Life,* (Alfred A. Knopf, 2004), p. 530.

159 Hillary Clinton, *Living History,* (First Scribner trade paperback edition 2004), p. 79.

160 Linda Tripp, *Press Conference.* Court House steps, July 1998.

161   Bill Clinton, *Larry King Live, CNN,* July 20, 1993. Also see: Bill Clinton, *My Life,* (Alfred A. Knopf, 2004), p. 530.

162   "What's the Rush? Review & Outlook," *Wall Street Journal....* July 20, 1993.

163   Chris Ruddy, "Ex-Chief: Politics Kept FBI Off Foster Case," *New York Post,* February 3, 1994.

164   *White House Press Office,* July 20, 1993.

165   Bill Clinton, *My Life,* (Alfred A. Knopf, 2004), p. 530.

166   Bill Clinton, *White House Press Release* (Remarks by the President), July 20, 1993.

167   Remarks by the President in Nomination of Judge Louis Freeh as Director of the FBI, *White House Press Release,* July 20, 1993.

168   "FBI Memo Cites Fund Probe Pressure," *Associated Press,* May 18, 2000.

169   Louis Freeh, "Ex-FBI Chief On Clinton's Scandals," *CBS 60 Minutes,* Oct. 6, 2005.

170   *White House Press Briefing,* July 21, 1993.

171   *White House Press Briefing,* July 21, 1993.

172   Kenneth W. Starr, Independent Counsel, *Report on the Death of Vincent W. Foster,* October 10, 1997. p. 72 [209] Rolla OIC 2/9/95, at 27. Investigator Braun 302. 2/7/95, at 8.

173   Kenneth W. Starr, Independent Counsel, *Report on the Death of Vincent W. Foster,* October 10, 1997, p. 72 [208] USPP Evidence /Property Control Receipt (Rolla) at 1-2.

174   Kenneth W. Starr, Independent Counsel, *Report on the Death of Vincent W. Foster,* October 10, 1997, p.72 [210] OIC Doc. No. DC-210-2620.

175   Kenneth W. Starr, Independent Counsel, *Report on the Death of Vincent W. Foster,* October 10, 1997, p.93.

176   "Progress of the investigation into Whitewater Development Corporation and Related Matters and Recommendations for Future Funding Report." *Senate Whitewater Committee,* 104-204, p.11.

177   Jonathan Strong, "President Obama snubs Issa on first major document deadline," *Daily Caller,* February 1, 2011.

178   Robert B. Fiske, Jr., Special Prosecutor, *Fiske Report,* June 30, 1994, p. 31.

179   Hillary Clinton, *Living History,* (First Scribner trade paperback edition 2004), p. 175.

180   Hillary Clinton, *Living History,* (First Scribner trade paperback edition 2004), p. 163.

181   Bill Clinton, *White House Press Briefing,* July 21, 1993.

182   Hillary Clinton, *Living History,* (First Scribner trade paperback edition 2004), p. 219.

183   Hillary Clinton, *Living History,* (First Scribner trade paperback edition 2004), p. 297.

184   *White House Press Briefing,* July 22, 1993.

185   *White House Press Briefing,* July 22, 1993.

186   Michael Isikoff, "Park Police to Conduct Inquiry 'Routine' Probe Set on Foster's Death," *Washington Post,* July 27, 1993.

187   Kenneth W. Starr, Independent Counsel, *Report on the Death of Vincent W. Foster,* October 10, 1997 p. 7 [11] Summary Report by William F. Clinger (Aug. 12, 1994) at 6.

188   Kenneth W. Starr, Independent Counsel, *Report on the Death of Vincent W. Foster*, October 10, 1997, p. 44.

189   Robert B. Fiske, Jr., Special Prosecutor, *Fiske Preliminary Report*, June 30, 1994, p.33.

190   Kenneth W. Starr, Independent Counsel, *Report on the Death of Vincent W. Foster*, October 10, 1997, p. 44.

191   Kenneth W. Starr, Independent Counsel, *Report on the Death of Vincent W. Foster*, October 10, 1997, p. 75 [221] OIC, 2/16/95, at 17.

192   Kenneth W. Starr, Independent Counsel, *Report on the Death of Vincent W. Foster*, October 10, 1997, p. 14, Lee Report at 485.

193   Kenneth W. Starr, Independent Counsel, *Report on the Death of Vincent W. Foster*, October 10, 1997, p.71 [206] .

194   Robert B. Fiske, Jr., Special Prosecutor, *Fiske Report*, June 30, 1994, p. 48.

195   Starr Referral, Supplemental Materials, *Part III* p. 4276.

196   Bill Clinton, *My Life*, (Alfred A. Knopf, 2004), p. 606.

197   Bill Clinton, *My Life*, (Alfred A. Knopf, 2004), p. 640.

198   Hillary Clinton, *Living History*, (First Scribner trade paperback edition 2004), p. 244.

199   Hillary Clinton, *Living History*, (First Scribner trade paperback edition 2004), p. 439.

200   *Final Report of Special Committee to Investigate Whitewater*, January 22, 1996, p. 97-98.

201   Bill Clinton, *White House Press Briefing,* July 21, 1993, 12:50 pm.

202   Chief of Staff Mack McLarty *White House Press Briefing*, July 21, 1993.

203   Dee Dee Myers, *White House Press Briefing*, July 22, 1993.

204   George Stephanopoulos, *All Too Human,* (Little Brown and Company, 1999) p. 185.

205   Kenneth W. Starr, Independent Counsel, *Report on the Death of Vincent W. Foster,* October 10, 1997, p. 4.

206   Hillary Clinton, NBC's *Today Show*, January 27, 1998.

207   Al Kamen, "Clinton-era Filegate appears to have closed, 14 years on," *Washington Post*, March 10, 2010.

208   Bill Clinton, *White House Press Conference with President Robinson of the Republic Ireland,* June 13, 1996.

209   Bernie Nussbaum, 302, 6/8/95 at 6, Kenneth W. Starr, Independent Counsel, *Report on the Death of Vincent W. Foster,* p. 108. "Suddenly her boss Nussbaum recalled, "Foster's work effort decreased noticeably." Also see, Kenneth W. Starr, Independent Counsel, *Report on the Death of Vincent W. Foster*, October 10, 1997, p.108. See: how others abruptly remembered, that he "had seemed distressed."

210   Saul Alinsky, *Rules for Radicals*, (Vintage, October 23, 1989), p. 30, 34.

211   *Special Committee to Investigate Whitewater*, January 22, 1996, p. 4.

212   *Special Committee to Investigate Whitewater*, January 22, 1996 p. 4, (Heymann, 8/2/95 Hrg. P.53).

213   Saul Alinsky, *Rules for Radicals*, (Vintage, October 23, 1989), p. 30, 34.

214   Linda Tripp, *Starr Report, Part III,* p. 4276. See July 28, 1998, at p. 47.

215   Margaret Carlson*, Time Magazine* interview, 1993.

216   First Amendment –Religion and Expression, United States Constitution.

217 Edward Zehr, "The anatomy of a cover-up: Ruddy's new book explains the Foster fiasco," *The Washington Weekly,* September 29, 1997 via Newsmax.com. *CBS's 60 Minutes* would do an attack piece on the author.

218 Hillary Clinton, *Living History,* (First Scribner trade paperback edition 2004), p. 297.

219 Special Report: Whitewater Timeline, *Washington Post,* October 1993.

220 Special Report: Whitewater Timeline, *Washington Post,* September 1993.

221 Robert W. Ray, Independent Counsel, *Final Report of the Independent Counsel In Re: Madison Guaranty Savings & Loan Association,* January 5, 2001 See: The Clintons, the McDougals, and the Whitewater Development Company. p. 1.
Also see: Zachary A. Goldfarb, "Fannie Mae, Freddie Mac losing political support as U.S. reshapes housing finance system," *Washington Post,* August 7, 2010.

222 Robert W. Ray, Independent Counsel, *Final Report of the Independent Counsel In Re: Madison Guaranty Savings & Loan Association,* January 5, 2001. See: Volume III – Washington D.C. Investigation Part E: The Discovery and Removal of Documents from Vincent W. Foster's Jr. Office. p. 148, See H. Clinton 4/22/95 Depo. At 10-11. H. Clinton 4/25/98 Depo. At 50-51.

223 Hillary Clinton, *Living History,* (First Scribner trade paperback edition 2004), p. 214.

224 Ben Smith, "Hillary's Hammer Returns," *Politico,* April 8, 2007.

225 Saul Alinsky, *Rules for Radicals,* (Vintage, October 23), 1989 p. 129.

226 Sam Smith, "White House Beefs Up Online Rapid Response," *Huffingtonpost.com,* May 23, 2011. Also see: Devin Swyer, "Obama 'Attack Watch' Website to Help Supporters 'Fight Back,' *ABC News,* September 13, 2011.

227 Whitewater Special Report, Timeline, *Washington Post.*

228 Sally Bedell Smith, "Why Hillary Clinton let husband Bill seduce any woman in sight," *Extracted from The Love of Politics: Bill and Hillary Clinton: The White House Years, by Sally Bedell Smith, 2008.*

229 George Stephanopoulos, All *Too Human,* (Little Brown and Company, 1999), p. 226.

230 Dee Dee Myers, Press Secretary, ABC's *Nightline* and PBS's *Frontline,* December 2000.

231 Bio: Bruce R. Lindsey. Clinton Foundation.

232 John M. Broder and David Lauter, "Clinton Calls for Special Counsel to Probe Land Deal: Presidency: Aides say request for Reno to name investigator is designed to end 'barrage of innuendo' that may threaten agenda. First Family denies wrongdoing." *Los Angeles Times,* January 13, 1994.

233 Whitewater Special Report, Timeline, *Washington Post,* September 1993.

234 Stephen Labaton, "Whitewater Panel Delves Into Long-Sought Billing Records," *New York Times,* February 1996.

235 Bill Clinton, *My Life,* (Alfred A. Knopf, 2004), p. 587.

236 Bill Clinton, *My Life,* (Alfred A. Knopf, 2004), p.584.

237 Hillary Rodham Clinton, *Living History,* (First Scribner trade paperback edition 2003), p. 195.

238 Robert W. Ray, Independent Counsel, *Final Report of the Independent Counsel* In Re: Madison Guaranty Savings & Loan Associations), January 5, 2001. See: Volume III – Washington, D.C. Investigation, Appendix 3: White House's Non-Compliance

with Subpoena Requests for Electronically Maintained Documents. Introduction, p i.

239   Robert W. Ray, Independent Counsel, *Final Report of the Independent Counsel In Re: Madison Guaranty Savings & Loan Association,* January 5, 2001. See Volume II- Arkansas Investigation, Volume II, Part B, Chapter 3: Mrs. Clinton's Madison Guaranty Representation, p. 495. Also see: Jerry Seper, "Once-secret memos question Clinton's honesty," *Washington Times,* May 8, 2008. Also see: Jerry Seper, "Clinton records vanished after warning of 'very serious problems," *Washington Times,* May 12, 2008.

240   Linda Tripp, *Larry King Live, CNN,* February 16, 1999.

241   J.P Freire, "DOJ Voting Rights attorney resigns over Black Panther stonewalling," *Washington Examiner,* May 17, 2010.

242   "Rwanda: How the genocide happened," *BBC,* December 18, 2008.

243   Promoting Peace, *PBS's a news hour with Jim Lehrer,* Bill Clinton apologizes to Rwanda, March 25, 1998.

244   David Lauter, "Clinton's Counsel Nussbaum Resigns," *Los Angeles* Times, March 6, 1994. "White House Counsel Bernard Nussbaum resigned Saturday, bringing to an end a yearlong tenure marked by controversy and accusations that his zealous advocacy of Bill Clinton's interests had compromised the President's political standing."

245   Jane Sherburne, Clinton White House Special Counsel, *ABC's Nightline/ PBS's Frontline,* January 2001.

246   William Lajeunesse, "ATF Director Reassigned: U.S. Attorney Out Amid 'Fast and Furious' Uproar," *Fox News,* August 30, 2011. Also see: Issa Statement on Resignation of Arizona U.S. Attorney, Reassignment of ATF Director, *Committee on Oversight & Government Reform.* "… While the reckless disregard for safety that took place in Operation Fast and Furious certainly merits changes within the Department of Justice, the Oversight and Government Reform Committee will continue its investigation to ensure that blame isn't offloaded on just a few individuals for a matter that involved much higher levels of the Justice Department. There are still many questions to be answered about what happened in Operation Fast and Furious and who else bears responsibility, but these changes are warranted and offer an opportunity for the Justice Department to explain the role other officials and offices played in the infamous efforts to allow weapons to flow to Mexican drug cartels. I also remain very concerned by Acting Director Melson's statement that the Department of Justice is managing its response in a manner intended to protect its political appointees. Senator Grassley and I will continue to press the Department of Justice for answers in order to ensure that a reckless effort like Fast and Furious does not take place again."

247   "Eric Holder's Politics: His years at Clinton Justice don't inspire confidence," *Wall Street Journal,* December 4, 2008. "The first question revolves around Mr. Holder's role in Bill Clinton's pardon of fugitive financiers Marc Rich. Mr. Holder was involved. In 1999, President Clinton offered clemency to 16 Puerto Rican members of the terrorist FALN, despite a previous warning from Attorney General Janet Reno that the group posed an "ongoing threat" to U.S. security. Also see: Letter to Secretary of State Hillary Rodham Clinton, March 29, 2011. "On March 29th, the head of

the House Oversight Committee fired off a letter to Secretary of State Hillary Clinton over her agency's refusal to turn over documents and information about the ATF "gunwalking" scandal exposed by *CBS News*. "Given the gravity of this matter, this refusal is simply unacceptable," reads the letter from Rep. Darrell Issa (R-Calif.)."

248   "Linda Tripp, *Starr Report, Part III*, p. 4276, See July 28, 1998, p.48.

249   Saul Alinsky, *Rules for Radicals,* (Vintage, October 23, 1989), p. 25.

250   Stephen Labaton, "Hillary Clinton Turned $1,000 into $99,540 White House says," *New York Times*, March 30, 1994.

251   Maureen Dowd, "The Whitewater Affair: News Analysis: 'Sorry' as a Political Weapon in the TV Age," *New York Times*, April 23, 1994.

252   Lydia Saad, "Obama, Hillary Clinton Share "Most Admired" Billing," *Gallup*, December 26, 2008.

253   A.W.R. Hawkins, "America's Smartest Woman' Is Making Us Look Stupid," *Human Events* April 1, 2009. Also see: Ton Fitton, "Judicial Watch Gets Hillarycare Docs... After 5-year Legal Battle," *Biggovernment.com*, February 22, 2011.

254   Nicholas Kristof, "Obama the intellectual," *New York Times,* October 17, 2008. Also see: Steven Erlanger and Sheryl Gay Stolberg, "Surprise Nobel for Obama Stirs Praise and Doubts," *New York Times,* October 9, 2009.

255   Matthew Boyle, "GAO releases Obamacare waiver analysis, still no clear rhyme or reason to process," *The Daily Caller,* June 15, 2011.

256   Saul Alinsky, *Rules for Radicals*, (Vintage, October 23, 1989), p. 99.

257   Saul Alinsky, *Rules for Radicals*, (Vintage, October 23, 1989), p. 84.

258   Jeff Mason, "Hillary Clinton calls Bosnia sniper story a mistake," *Reuters,* March 25, 2008.

259   Jonathan Weisman, "Obama's Uncle and the Liberation of Auschwitz," *Washington Post,* May 27, 2008.

260   Priscilla Painton, "Clinton's People: Bruce Lindsey," *Time Magazine,* November 23, 1992.

261   Linda Tripp, *Starr Report, Part III,* June 30, 1998; p. 57-58.

262   Linda Tripp, *Starr Report, Part III,* June 30, 1998; p. 4045. See p. 57-58.

263   Robert Burns, "Linda Tripp conducting Pentagon Duties from Home," *Associated Press*, February 26, 1998.

264   U.S. Department of Defense. The Pentagon facts.

265   Greg Miller and Christi Parsons, "Leon Panetta is Obama's pick for CIA director," *Los Angeles Times,* January 6, 2009.

266   Lois Romano, "Gatekeepers of Hillaryland," *Washington Post*, June 21, 2007.

267   "Narrative PT. II: Initial Sexual Encounters, Overview of Monica Lewinsky's White House Employment," *Washington Post,* 1998.

268   "Lewinsky and the first lady," *Associated Press,* March 19, 2008. Also see: "Betty Currie: Innocent or enabler?" *BBC News,* February 10, 1999.

269   *Starr Report,* Evelyn Lieberman 1/30/98 GJ at 45. Also see Panetta 1/28/98 GJ at 143 describing precautions taken "to protect the President's office and protect his integrity," including preventing President from meeting alone with female acquaintances in circumstances that "could be misinterpreted". Also see: A Chronology: Key Moments In the Clinton Impeachment," *CNN,* September 29, 1998. Lieberman also

told The *New York Times* the move was "due to inappropriate and immature behavior and inattention to work."

270   Saul Alinsky, *Rules for Radicals*, (Vintage, October 23, 1989), p. 65.

271   Linda Tripp and Monica Lewinsky were not alone in receiving perks. During the Whitewater investigations after Webster Hubbell resigned from the Justice Department and was awaiting trial, he received seventeen consulting contracts totaling over $450,000 from President Clinton supporters. The independent counsel found that Hubbell "did little or no work for the money paid by his consulting clients." Vernon Jordan, who headed President Clinton's transition team, tried to secure jobs for both Hubbell and Lewinsky at Revlon. White House staffers Betty Currie and John Podesta also pitched in when they asked then United Nations Ambassador Bill Richardson to get Lewinsky a job.

272   Kenneth R. Bazinet, "Obama's Ex-Green Jobs Czar Lands Quickly," *New York Daily News,* September 9. 2009.

273   Ari Berman, "Van Jones Previews the American Dream Movement," *The Nation,* June 23, 2011.

274   Lloyd Grove, "Clinton's Human Shield," *Washington Post*, September 16, 1998; p. D01.

275   Richard Miniter, "What Clinton Didn't Do… and when he didn't do it," *Wall Street Journal*, September 27, 2006.

276   Louis J. Freeh, "Remember Khobar Towers, Nineteen American heroes still await American Justice," *Wall Street Journal,* May 20, 2003.

277   *The 9/11 Commission Report,* (Barnes & Noble Publishing, Inc. 2004) p. 48, also see 3. in Chapter 2. The Foundation of the New Terrorism: Usama Bin Ladin, "Declaration of War Against the American's Occupying the Land of the Two Holy Places," August 23, 1996.

278   Interview Osama bin Laden, with *ABC's* John Miller, *PBS*, May 1998.

279   *The 9/11 Commission Report,* (Barnes $ Noble Publishing Inc. 2004), p.59.

280   Lloyd Grove, "Clinton's Human Shield," *Washington Post*, September 16, 1998, p. D01.

281   OIC Report: Narrative V via the *New York Times on the web*, 1998.

282   Executive Order 12968—Access to Classified Information: From the 1995 Presidential Documents Online via GPO Access [frwais.access.gpo.gov] [DOCID:pd07au95_txt-20], [Page 1365-1373] August 2, 1995, p. 1369.

283   Andrew Morton, *Monica's Story*, (St. Martin's Press, 1999), p. 107.

284   Art Harris and Michael Isikoff, "Jessica Hahn, On the Defensive; Her Claim of Sexual Inexperience is Disputed," *Washington Post*, September 30, 1987. p. C1.

285   The Joint Civilian Orientation Conference media documents.

286   Linda Tripp, *Starr Report, Part III,* July 28, 1998, p. 4281, see p. 67.

287   Transcript: Bill Clinton and Gennifer Flowers –Audio Tapes, Joe Goulden, *Accuracy In Media*, March 20, 1992.

288   Peter Baker, "See Willey Tells of Clinton Advance," *Washington Post*, March 16, 1998 versus Tripp testimony. Also see: Linda's FBI interview in *Starr Report*. Also see: Michael Isikoff and Thomas Evan, "What do you do? Tell his boss? Kathleen

Willey's vivid account of her alleged encounter with Clinton," *Newsweek,* March 9, 1998.

289   Lee Smith, "Federal Trial Is a Starr Attraction," *Washington Post,* May 3, 1999; p. B1.

290   "The Willey Letters," *Washington Post*, Released on March 16, 1998.

291   Michael Isikoff, "A Twist in Jones v. Clinton," *Newsweek,* August 11, 1997.

292   "Actress Who Claimed Sex with Bill says IRS is Hounding her," *The New York Post*, January 13, 1999.

293   Carl Limbacher, "IRS Official to Judicial Watch: Clinton Enemies Were Audited," *Newsmax*, April 23, 2002.

294   "The IRS Gets Political: The taxman goes after campaign donors," Editorial, Wall Street Journal.

295   Andrew Morton, *Monica's Story,* (St. Martin's Press, 1999), p. 114-115.

296   Andrew Morton, *Monica's Story,* (St. Martin's Press, 1999), p, 121.

297   Andrew Morton, *Monica's Story,* (St. Martin's Press, 1999), p. 121.

298   Andrew Morton, *Monica's Story,* (St. Martin's Press, 1999), p. 124.

299   Monica Lewinsky, *Starr Report,* August 6, 1998, p. 796.

300   Monica Lewinsky, *Starr Report,* August 6, 1998.

301   "Fast and Furious" a "Catastrophic Disaster:" Border agents criticize weapons program," Chairman Darrell Issa, the House Oversight and Government Reform Committee, *CSPAN,* June 15, 2011. Also see: Michael A. Walsh, "Fast and Furious' gets hotter for Holder," *New York Post,* July 7, 2011. Also see: Stephen Dinan and Chuck Neubauer, "Issa: Obama admin intimidating witnesses in ATF gun probe," *Washington Times*, July 26, 2011.

302   Linda Tripp, *Larry King Live, CNN,* February 16, 1999.

303   David Steitfeld, "Before Scandal, Tripp Wrote Book Proposal on Clinton Administration," *Washington Post*, January 28, 1998; p D01.

304   Frank Greve, "Tripp Was Also taped and Nudged to Act," *Inquirer, Washington Bureau,* October 2, 1998.

305   Linda Tripp, *Starr Report, Part III,* July 28, 1998, p. 4280, see p. 60-61(referring to conversation with Bruce Lindsey).

306   *Starr Report*, September 9, 1998.

307   Toby Harnden, "Obama administration 'pressured Air Force general to change testimony," *The Telegraph,* September 16, 2011. Also see: Darren Samuelsohn, "Solyndra executives repeatedly invoke the Fifth," *Politico*, September 23, 2011. Also see: "White House Orders Review of Energy Department Loans in Wake of Solyndra Scandal," *Fox News*, October 28, 2011. "Subpoenaing the White House is a serious step that, unfortunately, appears necessary in light of the Obama administration's stonewall on Solyndra," they said in a statement, accusing the administration of not cooperating since the committee launched an investigation more than eight months ago. "What is the White House trying to hide from the American public? It is alarming for the Obama White House to cast aside its vows of transparency and block Congress from learning more about the roles that those in the White House and other members of the administration played in the Solyndra mess," they said. Also see: Dina Cappiello, "White House rebuffs subpoena on failed solar firm," *Associated Press*, November 4, 2011.

308   Willey says lawyer badgered her, *Associated Press*, May 1999.

309   David P. Schippers, *Sell Out: The Inside Story of President Clinton's Impeachment*, (Regnery Publishing 2000), p. 115.

310   Linda Tripp, *Starr Report, Part III,* July 28, 1998, p. 57.

311   Clinton and the Intern, Michael Isikoff, *Newsweek* (round up) February 2, 1998; p. 6.

312   Matt Drudge, "Tripp Turns on Clinton, Tells of Willey Episode," *Drudge Report* August 3, 1997. Also see: David Van Biema and Viveca Novak, "Clinton Crisis: Sparking the Scandal," *Time Magazine,* February 2, 1998.

313   Ex-Aide Subpoenaed in Paula Jones Case, *Los Angeles Times,* August 4, 1997. "A former White House aide says another former worker, who has been subpoenaed in the Paula Jones sex harassment case, told her that President Clinton made sexual advances toward her in the White House, Newsweek reported. Jones's lawyers subpoenaed the former worker, Kathleen E. Willey."

314   David Streitfeld, "The Art of Publishing Sensations," *Washington Post*, March 19, 1998. Also see: Roger Friedman, "The Devil Gets His Due: Michael Viner, RIP, *Showbiz 411,* August 11, 2009. "My favorite Viner anecdote, just so you get the flavor of the man: he had his rep call a hotel and lie about being from the accounting department of New York Magazine to get a journalist's itemized phone bill. They wanted a list of the writer's calls so they could figure out who his sources were. They got the list and called the sources! Some other great moments: he sued Heidi Fleiss for libel, and lost. During the trial he admitted on the stand to having an affair with a hooker. Nice. Author's note: Viner published the audio version of my first book collaboration, *The Kid Stays In the Picture,*" and I can vouch for Kathleen that when it comes to Viner, the truth is open for negotiations.

315   *Starr Report,* 845-DC-00000190 (letter); Tripp 7/16/98 GJ at 85-88. Also see: Narrative Footnotes. From the independent counsel Kenneth Starr's report to the House on President Clinton. 845-DC-00000190 (letter); Tripp 7/16/98 GJ at 85-88.

316   "Chronology Paula Jones Civil Suit," *New York Times,* 1998.

317   Linda Tripp, *Starr Report, Part III*, July 7, 1998, p. 4144, see p. 133.

318   Linda Tripp, *Starr Report, Part III,* July 28, 1998; p. 4287, see p. 97.

319   Linda Tripp, *Starr Report, Part III,* p. 4276, see July 28, 1998, p. 46.

320   Maxim Lott, "Obama Administration Fires ATF Whistleblower," *Fox Nation,* June 28, 2011.

321   "The Lewinsky Tapes," *Newsweek,* January 24, 1998.

322   Linda Tripp, *Starr Report, Part III,* July 29, 1998; see p. 70.

323   "Lewinsky urged Tripp to lie," *BBC News,* October 3, 1998. "Monica Lewinsky offered Linda Tripp money to lie about the former intern's affair with President Clinton, according to transcripts of their taped conversations. "I would be indebted to you for life," she said. "I would write you a cheque for the entire portion (of a condominium) I own in Australia." In the taped conversations, Monica Lewinsky also says she was told to deny an affair with the president. In the transcripts, Ms Lewinsky says someone told her: "It doesn't matter what anybody says, you just deny it." However, she does not say who the advice came from. She says she feared for her life if she did not sign an affidavit denying having an affair with the president. The

transcripts also reveal how Ms. Lewinsky became anxious as her affair with Bill Clinton became public. At one stage, Ms. Lewinsky says: "It's just too - it's too much for one person."

324   Linda Tripp, *Starr Report, Part III*, August 20, 1998; p. 4364 see p. 17.

325   Linda Tripp, *Starr Report, Part III*, July 28, 1998, p. 88-89. Also see: Linda Tripp: "I don't expect as I presume I can now look forward and anticipate that these [tapes] would one day be public, not through my doing, but through other ways, I suppose and that that was not my intention . For her [Lewinsky] or me."

326   Linda Tripp with Nancy Collins, "Linda Tripp, the George Interview," *George Magazine*, December/January 2001.

327   Linda Tripp, *Starr Report, Part III*, July 28, 1998, p. 4285, see p. 81.
      Also see: Linda Tripp, *Starr Report, Part III*, p. 4286, See July 28, 1998, p. 87. Linda also testified, "I've come to learn over time much more than I knew at the time—[their] own personal agenda that I was not really completely familiar with until the story [of President Clinton's affair with Monica Lewinsky] broke." Also see: Elisabeth Bumiller, "The President's Acquittal: The Agent; Tripp Friend Says She's Proud of her Role," *New York Times*, February 13, 1999.

328   Linda Tripp, *Starr Report, Part III*, p. 4364, August 20, 1998, see p. 17.

329   Peter Baker, "Linda Tripp Briefed Jones Team on Tapes, (after she had Federal immunity)" *Washington Post*, February 14, 1998, p. A01. "One reason she may have cooperated with the Jones camp, Moody (Linda's lawyer) said, was to avoid having to testify in a formal deposition about the Jones case, where Clinton's attorneys would have had the chance to grill Tripp as well. Tripp had been subpoenaed by Jones's lawyers, but may have been able to persuade them to withdraw it by submitting to a private interview. "My objective at the time was to get her out of being deposed and off their radar screen," Moody said."

330   Neely Tucker, "Barack Obama, Camelot's New Knight," *Washington Post*, January 29, 2008.

331   Bill Daley, "Obama's New Chief of Staff," *Associated Press*, January 6, 2011.
      Also see: "New Details Emerge About Sex Allegations Against Clinton," *CNN's All Politics*, January 23, 1998.

332   Jake Tapper, "Obama Offers Rahm Emanuel Job of White House Chief of Staff," *ABC News*, November 5, 2008.
      Also see: White House, President Clinton's senior policy adviser, Rahm Emanuel, *CNN Late Edition with Wolf Blitzer*, January 25, 1998.

333   James Carville with Tim Russert, *Meet the Press*, January 25, 1998.

334   Mary Bruce, "Hoffa on Tea Party: 'Let's Take These Sons of Bitches Out!'" *ABC News*, September 5, 2011.

335   Michael A. Memoli, "Obama: Occupy Wall Street protests show American's frustration," *Los Angeles Times*, October 6, 2011.
      Also see: Melissa Jenco, "Bill Clinton: Wall Street protests can stir 'positive debate,' *Chicago Tribune*, October 11, 2011. Also see: DJ Redman, "Occupy Wall Street, L.A. and Chicago Protests are Nothing More Than a Front for the Obama 2012 Reelection Campaign," *Conservative Daily*, October 3, 2011. Also see: Jim Hoft, "Nazis

and Communists Throw Their Support Behind Occupy Wall Street Movements," *Gateway pundit,* October 15, 2011.

336   *White House press conference,* January 26, 1998.

337   Monica S. Lewinsky's affidavit signed on Jan. 7, 1998, and submitted to Paula Jones lawyers on Jan. 16, 1998.

338   Bill Clinton, *The Oprah Winfrey Show,* June 22, 2004.

339   David Maraniss, "First Lady's Energy, Determination Bind a Power Partnership," *Washington Post,* February 1, 1998; p. A01.

340   "In Midst of Storm, Hillary Clinton Keeps Outwardly Calm," *New York Times, Politics,* January 27, 1998.

341   "The President under Fire;" Excerpts from Interview with Clinton on *NBC,* January 28, 1998.

342   Linday Barnes, "Suing the President: Ten years later, John Whithead looks back at Jones v. Clinton," *The Hook,* January 24, 2008.

343   Saul Alinsky, *Rules for Radicals,* (Vintage, October 23, 1989), p. 117.

344   Michael Isikoff and Evan Thomas with Mark Hosenball, Karen Breslau and Daniel Klaidman, "The Secret War," *Newsweek Magazine,* Special Report, February 9, 1998, p. 36.

345   Saul Alinsky, *Rules for Radicals,* (Vintage, October 23, 1989), p.130.

346   Carla Hall and Tami Abollah, "Private Eye to the Stars is Guilty," *Los Angeles Times,* May 16, 2008.

347   Jane Mayer, "Portrait of a Whistleblower," *New Yorker Magazine,* March 23, 1998.

348   "The Privacy Act of 1974," Justice Department, updated September 26, 2003.

349   "Defense Department Settles with Linda Tripp," *Associated Press,* November 3, 2003.

350   Josh Margolin, "Obama digging up dirt on potential opponent Chris Christie," *New York Post,* May 23, 2011.

351   Jane Mayer, "Ink," *New Yorker Magazine,* December 28, 1998.

352   OBL, *London's Al-Quds al-'Arabi,* February 23, 1998.

353   National Organization for Women website.

354   Mary Dejevsky, "M is for Monica: an A to Zippergate of the affair," *The Independent, UK,* August 4 1998.

355   Carol Lloyd, "Clinton Crisis, Gossip the most dangerous Drug of all," *Salon.com.* "First of all, chief snitch Linda Tripp – whose "evidence" amounts to gossip run amok -."

356   Angie Cannon, "For Starr, his chance to speak, will he reverse a poor standing? *Inquirer Washington Bureau,* November 19, 1998. "For the last year, Kenneth W. Starr has watched in near silence as his pursuit of a president launched criticism that he had become a sex-crazed, out-of-control prosecutor hurling the country toward unwanted impeachment hearings. Hillary Rodham Clinton called him part of a "vast, right-wing conspiracy" against her husband. Clinton stalwart James Carville said Starr came forth like the creature from the Black Lagoon."

357   David S. Morgan, "Breitbart: Weiner offering limited version of truth," *CBS News,* June 7, 2011.

358   Excerpt from OIC Tripp-Lewinsky tapes: "I don't know, Monica. It's just this nagging, awful feeling in the back of my head."

"What if I didn't have it?"

"Well, I know that. I'm just - I think it's a blessing you do. It would be your insurance policy down the road. Or it could never be needed, and you can throw it away. But I – I never, ever want to read about you going off the deep end because someone comes out and calls you a stalker or something and ... some, God Forbid, awful like that. And in this day and age... I don't - I don't trust anybody. Maybe I'm just being paranoid. If I am, indulge me."

359   John Diamond, "Contrasting pictures of Lewinsky from Pentagon, White House," *Associated Press*, January 1998. "A part of the White House strategy is to raise questions about the veracity of the woman who is heard telling a friend on a secretly recorded tape that she had sexual relations with the president. The issue of whether these encounters were real or fantasy, and whether Clinton or his close friend Vernon Jordan pressured Lewinsky to deny the affair in a sworn affidavit, lies at the center of controversy."

360   Sidney Blumenthal testimony, *Starr Report*, p. 185.

361   Paul W. Valentine, "Maryland Jury to Probe Tripp's taping," *Washington Post,* July 8, 1998; p. A14.

362   Garance Franke-Ruta, "ACORN Sues O'Keefe, Giles and Breitbart.com," *Washington Post,* September 23, 2009.

363   Toni Lacy and Paul W. Valentine, "Lack of Tapes Stymies Case Against Tripp," *Washington Post,* November 6, 1998; p. B1.

364   "1998: US embassies in Africa bombed," BBC, August 7, 2005.

365   Televised address, President Bill Clinton, August 18, 1998.

366   *Starr Report* excerpt, September 9, 1998, the historyplace.com.

367   The History Place-Impeachment of Bill Clinton.

368   "'Clinton Lewinsky Effect': Study Shows Students' Changing Views of Oral Sex," *Huffingtonpost.com,* updated June 6, 2010. "Sexual definitions, the researchers hypothesized, were inevitably shaped by President Clinton's famous "I did not have sexual relations with that woman" statement and the ensuing national discussion." Like President Clinton, adolescents and young adults often interpret these words with a degree of latitude, depending on whether they want to maintain an image of being sexually experienced or inexperienced," the report explained. "Unlike respondents in the previous samples, our respondents were adolescents after the Clinton-Lewinsky era, which our comparisons of data over time suggest may have been a turning point in conceptualizations of oral-genital contact. The dramatic and sudden shift in attitudes toward oral-genital contact can therefore be termed the Clinton-Lewinsky effect." Also see: "Is it Sex or isn't it? What young adults think about Oral "Sex,'" *Guttmacher Institute,* News Release, April 5, 2010.

369   Matt Drudge, "She Had Sex With Cigar: Media Struggles With Shocking New Claims of White House Affair," *Drudge Report*, August 22, 1998.

370   The New Goodnight Kiss: What you Don't Know about Teen Sex," *ABC's Good Morning America,* May 2009.

371   David W. Freeman, "Oral sex now main cause of oral cancer: Who faces biggest risk?" *CBC News Health Watch*, February 23, 2011. Also see: Centers for Disease and Prevention, April 14, 2011. Also see: "Swedish researcher finds resistant gonorrhea,"

The Local (Sweden), July 11, 2011. "Scientists have for the first time found a strain of gonorrhea bacteria that is resistant to treatment with antibiotics, reported Magnus Unemo, the Swedish scientist who isolated the strain, at a conference about sexually transmitted diseases in Ottawa, Canada."

372   "Colleges Victims Blame, Turn a Blind Eye to Sexual Assault," *NBC Today Show*, May 19, 2011.

373   "Full Transcript of NBC Dateline report on Juanita Broaddrick," Dateline *NBC*, January 1999. Also see: "An Open Letter to Hillary Clinton by Juanita Broaddrick, Do you remember?"
October 15, 2000. Also see: Keating Holland, "Poll: Strong majority do not want Clinton removed from office," *CNN*, January 11, 1999. Author's note: I've had the pleasure of meeting Juanita Broaddrick. She is credible.

374   Juanita Broadrick, "An Open Letter To Hillary Clinton," October 15, 2000.
"I remember it as though it was yesterday. I only wish that it were yesterday and maybe there would still be time to do something about what your husband, Bill Clinton, did to me. There was a political rally for Mr. Clinton's bid for governor of Arkansas. I had obligated myself to be at this rally prior to my being assaulted by your husband in April, 1978. I had made up my mind to make an appearance and then leave as soon as the two of you arrived. This was a big mistake, but I was still in a state of shock and denial. You had questioned the gentleman who drove you and Mr. Clinton from the airport. You asked him about me and if I would be at the gathering. Do you remember? You told the driver, "Bill has talked so much about Juanita", and that you were so anxious to meet me. Well, you wasted no time. As soon as you entered the room, you came directly to me and grabbed my hand. Do you remember how you thanked me, saying "we want to thank you for everything that you do for Bill". At that point, I was pretty shaken and started to walk off. Remember how you kept a tight grip on my hand and drew closer to me? You repeated your statement, but this time with a coldness and look that I have seen many times on television in the last eight years. You said, "Everything you do for Bill". You then released your grip and I said nothing and left the gathering. What did you mean, Hillary? Were you referring to my keeping quiet about the assault I had suffered at the hands of your husband only two weeks before? Were you warning me to continue to keep quiet? We both know the answer to that question ..."

375   William J. Bennett, "What We Know," *Wall Street Journal*, April 16, 1998.

376   House impeached Clinton, *CNN*, December 19, 1998.

377   Jack Shafer, "WikiLeaks, Hillary Clinton, and the Smoking Gun," *Slate*, November 29, 2010.

378   Full Transcript of *NBC Dateline* report on Juanita Broaddrick with Lisa Myers, 1999.

379   Linda Tripp, "I am You" speech via *CNN's Larry King Live*, transcript, December 1, 2003.

380   Linda Tripp, *Starr Report, Part III*, p. July 28, 1998, p. 71.

381   Saul Alinsky, *Rules for Radicals*, (Vintage, October 23, 1989), p. 128.

382   Eric Lichtblau, "Clinton Strikes Indictment deal; Case is dropped as President Admits to False testimony," *Los Angeles Times*, January 20, 2001, Part A, National Desk, p. 1.

383   Mark Sherman, "Berger to Plead Guilty to Taking Materials," *Associated Press,* April 1, 2005.

384   Former Clinton Aide Pleads Guilty to Taking Classified Doc, *Fox News*. April 3, 2005.

385   Robert W. Ray, Independent Counsel, *Final Report of the Independent Counsel*, March 6, 2001.

386   *United States Attorney's Manual, Title 9 § 9-27.220*. "The Principals of Federal Prosecution set forth, a two-step process for determining whether charges should be sought. First, a prosecutor must determine whether the evidence is sufficient. *Id.* Second, a prosecutor must determine whether the matter still warrants a prosecution. *Id.* Moreover, because President Clinton was central to the Independent Counsel's investigation under the jurisdictional mandate, the final report of that investigation must sufficiently detail President Clinton's conduct and the legal evaluation of that conduct. See H.R. Conf. Rep. No. 103-511, at 19-20 (1994) (the Conference Committee" consider[ed] to be crucial a discussion of the conduct of the person for whom the independent counsel was appointed to office").

      Here, the Independent Counsel's opinion that sufficient evidence existed to seek charges President Clinton is stated in this limited analytical context, and does not establish that a crime was in fact committed, which can only be done under our system of justice by a trier of fact after a constitutionally required trial, or by guilty plea. United States Attorneys' Manual, Title 1 § 1-7.530 (B). Also see, Robert Ray, *Final Report of the Independent Counsel*, March 6, 2002, p. 41-42.

387   Bill Clinton, *The Oprah Winfrey Show,* June 22, 2004.

388   Paul W. Valentine, "Tripp Not Done with Jury Probe," *Washington Post*, August 1, 1998, p.A11.

389   Helen Kennedy, "Md Prosecutors Drop Tripp Wiretapping Charges," *New York Daily News*, May 25, 2000.

390   Amy Wallace, "Face-Off: The Confounding Case of Marchioni v. Keyes," *Los Angeles Magazine,* September 2003.

391   Linda Tripp Press release, see marinkapeschmann.com/endnotes

392   Richard Poe, "The Idiot's Guide to Chinagate," *Newsmax,* May 27, 2003.

393   Joseph Murtha, "The Long and Winding Road Continues,' *Linda Tripp.com*. See marinkapeschmann.com/endnotes.

394   Josh Getlin, "Hillary Clinton Formally Announces Senate Campaign," *Los Angeles Times,* February 7, 2000.

395   Liz Smith, "Tripp Hustles Book Without Goldberg," *Newsday*, July 17, 2000.."I suppose you thought you had heard the last of Linda Tripp, the woman who blew the whistle on Monica Lewinsky and President Clinton. But no. An independent agent in Los Angeles, Mike Hamilburg, is hustling a book proposition from Linda and claims she could actually produce her work before the November election. That's a very dubious timetable."

396   The Reliable Source, Lloyd Grove, *Washington Post,* July 28, 2000; Page C03.

397   LindaTripp.com. See marinkapeschmann.com/endnotes

398   "Linda Tripp Says She Has No Regrets," *Associated Press*, December 11, 2000.
       Also see: "No Regrets for Linda Tripp," *Newmax.com,* December 12, 2000.

399   Joseph F. Conner, "FALN, Holder, and Obama: The Price Paid by One 'Ordinary
       American,' Human Events, August 20, 2008. Also see: "Clinton's Rosenberg
       Case, Before we "move on,"" *National Review*, March 19, 2001.Also see: Jessica
       Reaves, "Pardongate Play-by-Play," *Time Magazine,* February 27, 2001. Also see:
       Jad Mouawad, "Book on Marc Rich Details His Iran Oil Deals," *New York Times*,
       October 15, 2009. Also see: "Tripp: I Could Have Spared Bill Pardongate Woes,"
       Newsmax.com, February 25, 2001 reporting interview Linda Tripp had with *Fox
       News'* Hannity and Colmes.

400   Nancy Collins, *CBS's Entertainment Tonight,* January 12, 2001. "In fact she [Linda
       Tripp] is a million dollars in debt to her lawyers." Also see: Linda Tripp Interview
       with Nancy Collins, *ABC News 20/20,* January 11, 2001. Author's note: A col-
       league at *ABC's 20/20* (when I called to warn her) confirmed what I knew, that
       although Linda's criminal indictment was dropped long ago, her criminal lawyer
       Joe Murtha was still running the interview and was indeed 'very controlling.' Also
       see: Linda Tripp Interview with Nancy Collins, *ABC News 20/20*, January 11, 2001.
       Also see: John Solomon, "In Journalism, "Exclusive Isn't So Exclusive Any More,"
       NPR, April 14, 2001. "Throughout the programming day of February 21st, Fox
       News Channel ran a promo promising an "exclusive" interview with Linda Tripp on
       its talk show "*Hannity and Colmes.*"Fox made that claim despite the fact that Tripp
       had been interviewed by Charles Gibson the day before on ABC's "Good Morn-
       ing America". It was also a month after ABC's newsmagazine *20/20* had promoted
       its own interview with Tripp with correspondent Nancy Collins as an "Exclusive".
       Exclusive – even though Collins also interviewed Tripp for the December issue of
       George magazine, which of course prominently slapped "Exclusive" on its cover. In
       journalism, the word exclusive isn't all that exclusive any more. Also see: Liz Smith,
       "Tripp Tells Shocking Stuff: George Magazine Interview," *Newsday,* December 18,
       2000. Also see: Nancy Collins on *CNN's Larry King,* "Linda Tripp Returns: What
       Does She have to Say?" Aired December 19, 2000.

401   Linda Tripp with Nancy Collins, "Linda Tripp, the George Interview, I'd Do It All
       Over Again," *George Magazine,* December/January 2001.

402   Linda Tripp with Nancy Collins, "Linda Tripp, the George Interview, I'd Do It All
       Over Again," *George Magazine,* December/January 2001.

403   Linda Tripp, *Starr Report, Part III,* June 30, 1998; p. 4045, see p. 57-58.

404   David Pace, "Linda Tripp Fired From Pentagon Job," *Associated Press,* January 19,
       2001. "Linda Tripp, whose secret tape recordings spurred the impeachment of
       President Clinton, was fired Friday after she refused to resign like other political
       appointees."

405   "Broke, Tripp seeks donations," *New York Post,* August 24, 2001. Also see: Marianne
       Means, "Linda Tripp just won't go away, "*Hearst Newspapers,* June 28, 2001."She
       laments in her letter that she owes $2 million in legal fees and "I now find myself
       with no money for rent, transportation, food, heat and utilities and other basics of

life. In her fund-raising appeal she says, "What I have suffered and endured for telling the truth I would not wish on even my worst enemy. . . . (But) "in the end, if I have nothing else, I have my integrity. I am not defeated."

406   "Defense Department settles with Linda Tripp," *Associated Press,* November 3, 2003.
407   Amplified Bible Footnotes, Numbers 20:12.
408   White House memo addressed to Harold Ickes, January 27, 1998. See marinkapeschmann.com/endnotes
409   Harold Ickes, *Starr Report Part I*, June 10, 1989, p. 1535 at p.69.
410   President George H.W. Bush, *Executive Order 12731* of October 17, 1990, "The Principles of Ethical Conduct For Government Officers and Employees."

Made in the USA
Lexington, KY
17 October 2013